W9-BLR-336

Statistical Methods for Psychology

EIGHTH EDITION

David C. Howell
The University of Vermont

Prepared by

David C. Howell
The University of Vermont

WADSWORTH
CENGAGE Learning

Australia • Brazil • Japan • Korea • Mexico • Singapore • Spain • United Kingdom • United States

For product information and technology assistance, contact us at
**Cengage Learning Customer & Sales Support,
1-800-354-9706**

For permission to use material from this text or product, submit all requests online at **www.cengage.com/permissions**
Further permissions questions can be emailed to **permissionrequest@cengage.com**

ISBN-13: 978-1-133-48932-0
ISBN-10: 1-133-48932-X

Wadsworth
20 Davis Drive
Belmont, CA 94002-3098
USA

Cengage Learning is a leading provider of customized learning solutions with office locations around the globe, including Singapore, the United Kingdom, Australia, Mexico, Brazil, and Japan. Locate your local office at: **www.cengage.com/global**

Cengage Learning products are represented in Canada by Nelson Education, Ltd.

To learn more about Wadsworth, visit **www.cengage.com/wadsworth**

Purchase any of our products at your local college store or at our preferred online store **www.cengagebrain.com**

Printed in the United States of America
1 2 3 4 5 6 7 15 14 13 12 11

Table of Contents

General Notes

These solutions were checked using a variety of calculators and computer software. Answers often differ (sometimes a surprising amount) depending on how many decimal places the calculator or program carries. It is important not to be too concerned about differences, especially ones in the second or third decimal place, which may be attributable to rounding (or the lack thereof) in intermediate steps.

Although I do not provide detailed answers to all discussion questions, for reasons given elsewhere, I have provided pointers for what I am seeking for many (though not all) of them. I hope that these will facilitate using these items as a basis of classroom discussion.

Chapter 1 – Basic Concepts

1.1   The entire student body of your college or university would be considered a population under any circumstances in which you want to generalize *only* to the student body of your college or university and no further.

1.3   The students of your college or university are a nonrandom sample of U.S. students, for example, because all U.S. students do not have an equal chance of being included in the sample.

1.5   Independent variables: (a) First grade students who attended Kindergarten versus those who did not. (b) Seniors, Masters, Submasters, and Juniors as categories of marathon runners. Dependent variables: (a) Social-adjustment scores assigned by first-grade teachers. (b) Time to run 26 miles, 385 yards.

1.7   Continuous variables: (a) Length of gestation. (b) Typing speed in words/minute. (c) Level of serotonin in a particular subcortical nucleus.

1.9   The planners of a marathon race would like to know the average times of Senior, Master, Submaster, and Junior runners so as to facilitate planning for handling the finish line.

1.11   Categorical data: (a) The number of Brown University students in an October, 1984, referendum voting For and the number voting Against the university's stockpiling suicide pills in case of nuclear disaster. (b) The number of students in a small Midwestern college who are white, African-American, Hispanic-American, Asian, Native American, Alaskan Native, or Other. (c) One year after an experimental program to treat alcoholism, the number of participants who are "still on the wagon", "drinking without having sought additional treatment", or "again under treatment".

1.13   Children's scores in an inner-city elementary school could be reported numerically (a measurement variable), or the children could be categorized as Bluebirds ($X > 90$), Robins ($X = 70$–90), or Cardinals ($X < 70$).

1.15   For adults of a given height and sex, weight is a ratio scale of body weight, but it is *at best* an ordinal scale of physical health.

1.17   Speed is probably a much better index of motivation than of learning.

1.19   **a.** The final grade point averages for low-achieving students taking courses that interested them could be compared with the averages of low-achieving students taking courses that don't interest them.

            b. The quality of communication could be compared for happily versus unhappily married couples.

1.21 For a synonym of "independent variable" see http://answers.yahoo.com/question/index?qid=20100919185852AAmMc57

1.23 An interesting study of the health effects of smoking in China can be found at http://www.berkeley.edu/news/media/releases/2005/09/04_smoking.shtml

Chapter 2 - Describing and Exploring Data

2.1 Children's recall of stories:

a.

Children's "and then...s"	Frequency
10	1
11	1
12	1
15	3
16	4
17	6
18	10
19	7
20	7
21	3
22	2
23	2
24	1
31	1
40	1

Distribution of And-Then statements for children

b. unimodal and positively skewed

2.3 The problem with making a stem-and-leaf display of the data in Exercise 2.1 is that almost all the values fall on only two leaves if we use the usual 10s' digits for stems.

Stem	Leaf
1	01255566667777778888888889999999
2	000000011122334
3	1
4	0

And things aren't much better even if we double the number of stems.

Stem	Leaf
1*	012
1.	555666677777788888888889999999
2*	000000011122334
2.	
3*	1
3.	
4*	0

Best might be to use the units digits for stems and add HI and LO for extreme values

3

Stem	Leaf
5	555
6	6666
7	7777777
8	8888888888
9	9999999
10	0000000
11	111
12	22
13	33
14	4
HI	31 40

2.5   Stem-and-leaf diagram of the data in Exercises 2.1 and 2.4:

Children		Adults
	0*	1
	0t	34
	0f	55
	0s	7777
	0.	88889999999
10	1*	00000000111111
2	1t	222223
555	1f	4444555
7777776666	1s	667
7777778888888888	1.	
1110000000	2*	
3322	2t	
4	2f	
	2s	
	2.	
40 31	Hi	

4

2.7 Invented bimodal data:

Score	Freq
1	2
2	3
3	5
4	10
5	15
6	19
7	16
8	12
9	10
10	15
11	19
12	19
13	16
14	13
15	8
16	4
17	3
18	2
19	1
20	1

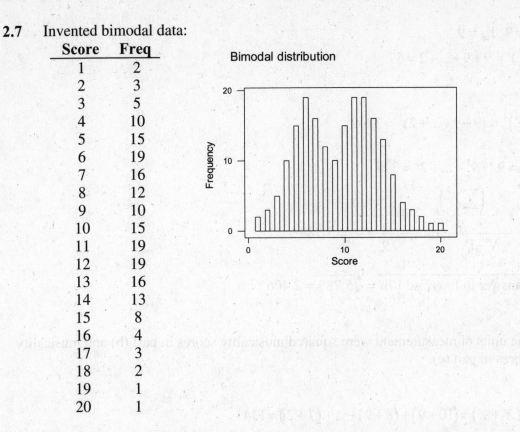

2.9 The first quartile for males is approximately 77, whereas for females it is about 80. The third quartiles are nearly equal for males and females, with a value of 87.

2.11 The shape of the distribution of number of movies attended per month for the next 200 people you met would be positively skewed with a peak at 0 movies per month and a sharp drop-off to essentially the baseline by about 5 movies per month.

2.13 Stem-and-leaf for ADDSC

Stem	Leaf
2.	69
3*	0344
3.	56679
4*	00023344444
4.	5566677888899999
5*	00000000011223334
5.	55677889
6*	00012234
6.	55556899
7*	0024
7.	568
8*	
8.	55

2.15 **a.** $Y_1 = 9$ $Y_{10} = 9$

     b. $\sum Y = 9 + 9 + ... + 2 = 57$

2.17 **a.** $(\sum Y)^2 = (9 + 9 + ... + 2)^2 = 3249$

$$\sum Y^2 = 9 + 9^2 + ... + 2^2 = 377$$

     b. $\dfrac{\sum Y^2 - \dfrac{\left(\sum Y^2\right)}{N}}{N-1} = \dfrac{460 - \dfrac{3249}{10}}{9} = 5.789$

     c. $\sqrt{\text{answer to Exercise 17b}} = \sqrt{5.789} = 2.406$

     d. The units of measurement were squared musicality scores in part (b) and musicality scores in part (c).

2.19 **a.**

$$\Sigma(X + Y) = (10 + 9) + (8 + 9) + ... + (7 + 2) = 134$$
$$\Sigma X + \Sigma Y = 77 + 57 = 134$$

     b.

$$\Sigma XY = 10(9) + 3(8) + ... + 3(7) = 460$$
$$\Sigma X \Sigma Y = (77)(57) = 4389$$

     c.

$$\Sigma CX = \Sigma 3X = 3(10) + 3(8) + ... + 3(7) = 231$$
$$C\Sigma X = 3(77) = 231$$

     d.

$$\Sigma X^2 = 10^2 + 8^2 + ... + 7^2 = 657$$
$$(\Sigma X)^2 = 77^2 = 5929$$

2.21 The results in Exercise 2.20 support the sequential processing hypothesis.

2.23 The data are not likely to be independent observations because the subject is probably learning the task over the early trials, and later getting tired as the task progresses. Thus responses closer in time are more likely to be similar than responses further away in time.

2.25 The amount of shock that a subject delivers to a white participant does not depend upon whether or not that subject has been insulted by the experimenter. On the other hand, black participants do suffer when the experimenter insults the subject.

6

2.27   AIDS cases among people aged 13–29 in U.S. population (in thousands):

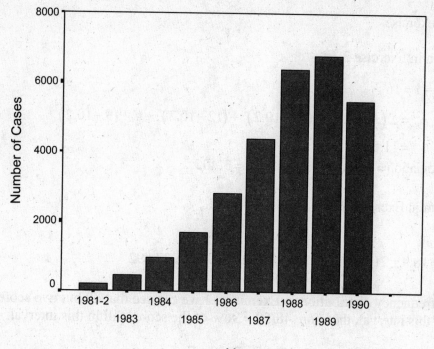

2.29   There is a strong increase in age at marriage, although the difference between males and females remains about the same. It is likely that what we are seeing is an increase in the percentage of couples living together without marrying. They finally get around to marrying about 5 years later than they used to.

2.31   The mean falls above the median.

2.33   Rats running a straight alley maze:

$$\bar{X} = \frac{\sum X}{N} = \frac{320}{15} = 21.33 \; ; \text{Median} = 21$$

2.35   Multiplying by a constant:

Original data (X):   8   3   5   5   6   2 $\bar{Y} = 4.83$
                                                                Median = 5
                                                                Mode = 5

Transformed data (Y = 3X)   24   9   15   15   18   6 $\bar{Y} = 14.5$
                                                                Median = 15
                                                                Mode = 15

$$3\,\bar{X} = \bar{Y}$$ $$3(\text{Med}_x) = \text{Med}_y$$ $$3(\text{Mo}_x) = \text{Mo}_y$$
$$3(4.83) = 14.5$$ $$3(5) = 15$$ $$3(5) = 15$$
$$14.5 = 14.5$$ $$15 = 15$$ $$15 = 15$$

7

2.37 They look just the way I would have expected.

2.39 Computer exercise

2.41 For the data in Exercise 2.4:

range $= 17 - 1 = 16$

variance $= s_X^2 = \Sigma\left(X - \bar{X}\right)^2 = \left(10-10.2\right)^2 + \left(12-10.2\right)^2 + \ldots + \left(9-10.2\right)^2$
$$= 11.592$$
standard deviation $= s_X = \sqrt{s_X^2} = \sqrt{11.592} = 3.405$

2.43 For the data in Exercise 2.1:

The interval:
$$\bar{X} \pm 2s_X = 18.9 \pm 2\left(4.496\right) = 18.9 \pm 8.992 = 9.908 \text{ to } 27.892$$

From the frequency distribution in Exercise 2.1 we can see that all but two scores (31 and 40) fall in this interval, therefore $48/50 = 96\%$ of the scores fall in this interval.

2.45 Original data: 5   8   3   8   6   9   9   7

$s_1 = 2.1$
If $X_2 = cX_1$, then $s_2 = cs_1$ and we want $s_2 = 1.00$

$s_2 = cs_1$
$1 = c(2.1)$
$c = 1/(2.1)$

Therefore we want to divide the original scores by 2.1

$X_2 = \dfrac{X_1}{2.1}$ 2.381   3.809   1.428   3.809   2.857   4.286   4.286   3.333

$s_2 = 1$

2.47 Boxplot for ADDSC [Refer to stem-and-leaf in Exercise 2.15]:

Median location $= (N + 1)/2 = (88 + 1)/2 = 89/2 = 44.5$
Median $= 50$
Hinge location $= (\text{Median location} + 1)/2 = (44 + 1)/2 = 45/2 = 22.5$
Hinges $= 44.5$ and 60.5
H-spread $= 60.5 - 44.5 = 16$
 Inner fences $= \text{Hinges} \pm 1.5*(\text{H-spread})$
                     $= 60.5 + 1.5(16) = 60.5 + 24 = 84.5$
        and $= 44.5 - 1.5(16) = 44.5 - 24 = 20.5$
 Adjacent values $= 26$ and 78

8

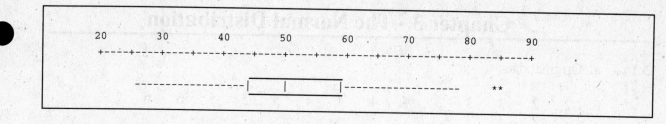

```
          20        30        40        50        60        70        80        90
          +----+----+----+----+----+----+----+----+----+----+----+----+----+----+----+

                    --------------------   -----------------           **
                                        |        |        |
                                        ----------------
```

2.49 Coefficient of variation for Appendix Data Set
$s/\bar{X} = 0.8614/2.456 = 0.351$

2.51 10% trimmed means of data in Table 2.6

   3.13 3.17 3.19 3.19 3.20 3.20 3.22 3.23 3.25 3.26

   3.27 3.29 3.29 3.30 3.31 3.31 3.34 3.34 3.36 3.38

Ten percent trimming would remove the two extreme observations at either end of the distribution, leaving

   3.19 3.19 3.20 3.20 3.22 3.23 3.25 3.26

   3.27 3.29 3.29 3.30 3.31 3.31 3.34 3.34

$$\bar{X} = \frac{52.28}{16} = 32.675$$

In this case the trimmed mean is very close to the untrimmed mean (3.266).

2.53 Reaction times when stimulus was present or absent.

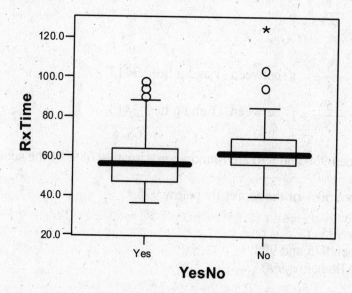

2.55 This is an Internet search that has no fixed answer.

9

Chapter 3 - The Normal Distribution

3.1   **a.** Original data:

1   2   2   3   3   3   4   4   4   4   5   5   5   6   6   7

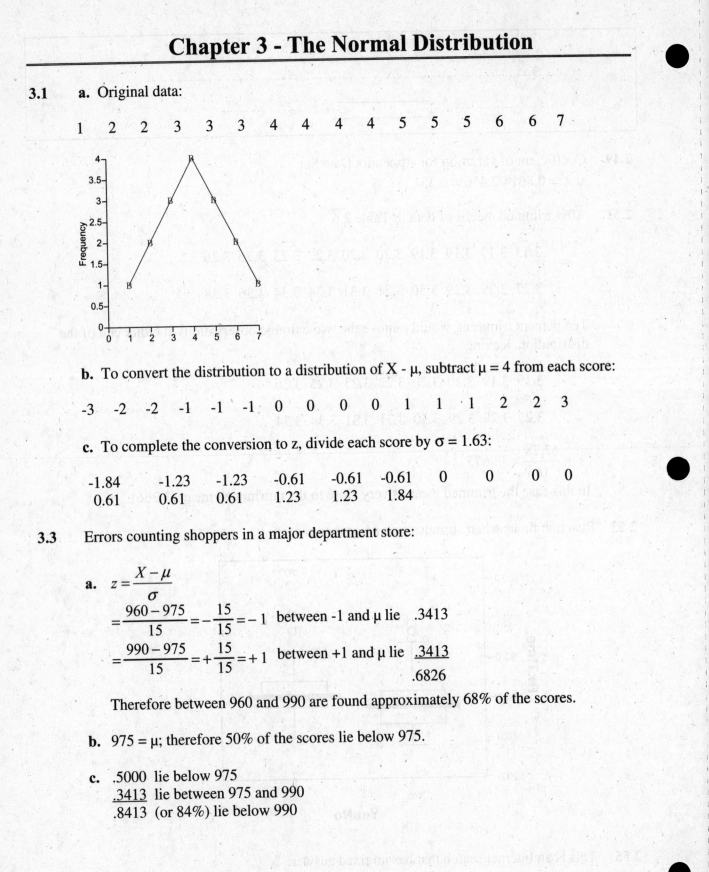

b. To convert the distribution to a distribution of X - μ, subtract μ = 4 from each score:

-3 -2 -2 -1 -1 -1 0 0 0 0 1 1 1 2 2 3

c. To complete the conversion to z, divide each score by σ = 1.63:

-1.84   -1.23   -1.23   -0.61   -0.61 -0.61   0   0   0   0
0.61   0.61   0.61   1.23   1.23   1.84

3.3   Errors counting shoppers in a major department store:

a. $z = \dfrac{X - \mu}{\sigma}$

$= \dfrac{960 - 975}{15} = -\dfrac{15}{15} = -1$ between -1 and μ lie .3413

$= \dfrac{990 - 975}{15} = +\dfrac{15}{15} = +1$ between +1 and μ lie <u>.3413</u>
                                                  .6826

Therefore between 960 and 990 are found approximately 68% of the scores.

b. 975 = μ; therefore 50% of the scores lie below 975.

c. .5000 lie below 975
     <u>.3413</u> lie between 975 and 990
     .8413 (or 84%) lie below 990

10

3.5   The supervisor's count of shoppers:

$$z = \frac{X - \mu}{\sigma}$$

$$= \frac{950 - 975}{15}$$

$$= -1.67$$

X to ±1.67 = 2(.0475) = .095; therefore 9.5% of the time scores will be at least this extreme.

3.7   They would be equal when the two distributions have the same standard deviation.

3.9   Next year's salary raises:

a.

$$z = \frac{X - \mu}{\sigma}$$

$$-1.2817 = \frac{X - 2000}{400}$$

$$\$2512.68 = X$$

10% of the faculty will have a raise equal to or greater than $2,512.68.

b.

$$z = \frac{X - \mu}{\sigma}$$

$$-1.645 = \frac{X - 2000}{400}$$

$$\$1342 = X$$

The 5% of the faculty who haven't done anything useful in years will receive no more than $1,342 each, and probably don't deserve that much.

3.11   Transforming scores on diagnostic test for language problems:

X_1 = original scores	$\mu_1 = 48$	$\sigma_1 = 7$
X_2 = transformed scores	$\mu_2 = 80$	$\sigma_2 = 10$

$$\sigma_2 = \sigma_1 / C$$

$$10 = 7 / C$$

$$C = 0.7$$

11

Therefore to transform the original standard deviation from 7 to 10, we need to divide the original scores by .7. However dividing the original scores by .7 divides their mean by .7.

$$\bar{X}_2 = \bar{X}_1 / 0.7 = 48 / .7 = 68.57$$

We want to raise the mean to 80. $80 - 68.57 = 11.43$. Therefore we need to add 11.43 to each score.

$$\bar{X}_2 = \bar{X}_1 0.7 + 11.43$$

$X_2 = X_1/0.7 + 11.43$. [This formula summarizes the whole process.]

3.13 October 1981 GRE, all people taking exam:

$$z = \frac{X - \mu}{\sigma}$$

$$= \frac{600 - 489}{126}$$

$$= 0.88 \quad p(\text{larger portion}) = 0.81$$

A GRE score of 600 would correspond to the 81st percentile.

3.15 October 1981 GRE, all seniors and nonenrolled college graduates:

$$z = \frac{X - \mu}{\sigma} \qquad\qquad z = \frac{X - \mu}{\sigma}$$

$$= \frac{600 - 507}{118} \qquad 0.6745 = \frac{X - 507}{118}$$

$$= 0.79 \quad p = .785 \qquad 586.591 = X$$

For seniors and nonenrolled college graduates, a GRE score of 600 is at the 79th percentile, and a score of 587 would correspond to the 75th percentile.

3.17 GPA scores:

$$N = 88 \quad \bar{X} = 2.46 \quad s = 0.86 \quad \text{[calculated from data set]}$$

$$z = \frac{X - \bar{X}}{s}$$

$$0.6745 = \frac{X - 2.46}{0.86}$$

$$3.04 = X$$

The 75th percentile for GPA is 3.04.

12

3.19 There is no meaningful discrimination to be made among those scoring below the mean, and therefore all people who score in that range are given a *T* score of 50.

3.21 Weight gain data

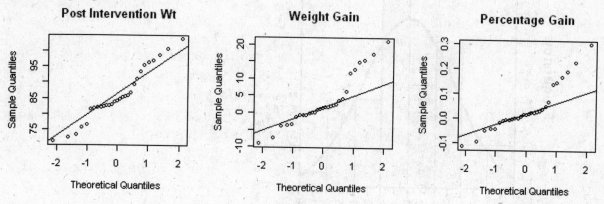

None of these is very close to normal, but the post intervention weight is closest.

3.23 I would first draw 16 scores from a normally distributed population with $\mu = 0$ and $\sigma = 1$. Call this variable z1. The sample (z1) would almost certainly have a sample mean and standard deviation that are not 0 and 1. Then I would create a new variable z2 = z1-mean(z1). This would have a mean of 0.00. Then I would divide z2 by sd(z1) to get a new distribution (z3) with mean = 0 and sd = 1. Then make that variable have a st. dev. of 4.25 by multiplying it by 4.25. Finally add 16.3 (the new mean). Now the mean is exactly 16.3 and the standard deviation is exactly 4.25.

3.25 SAT Data

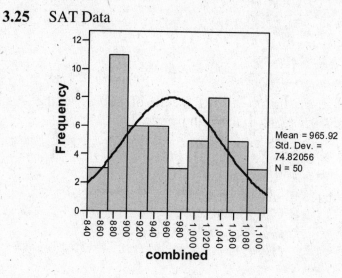

Mean = 965.92
Std. Dev. =
74.82056
N = 50

13

The data are actually bimodal, with probably too few scores at the extremes.

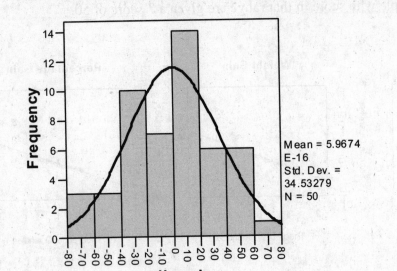

Mean = 5.9674
E-16
Std. Dev. =
34.53279
N = 50

These data are much more normally distributed. As we will see in Chapter Nine, there are two kinds of students who take the SAT, depending on where they live. It the East most students take it. In the West, students applying to high ranking eastern schools take it. This leads to the bimodal distribution in the adjusted scores.

Chapter 4 – Sampling Distributions and Hypothesis Testing

4.1   Was last night's game an NHL hockey game?

   a. Null hypothesis: The game was actually an NHL hockey game.

   b. On the basis of that null hypothesis I expected that each team would earn somewhere between 0 and 6 points. I then looked at the actual points and concluded that they were way out of line with what I would expect if this were an NHL hockey game. I therefore rejected the null hypothesis.

4.3   A Type I error would be concluding that I had been shortchanged when in fact I had not.

4.5   The critical value would be that amount of change below which I would decide that I had been shortchanged. The rejection region would be all amounts less than the critical value—i.e., all amounts that would lead to rejection of H_0.

4.7   Was the son of the member of the Board of Trustees fairly admitted to graduate school?

$$z = \frac{X - \mu}{\sigma}$$

$$z = \frac{490 - 650}{50}$$

$$= -3.2$$

z score	p
3.00	0.0013
3.20	0.0007
3.25	0.0006

The probability that a student drawn at random from those properly admitted would have a GRE score as low as 490 is .0007. I suspect that the fact that his mother was a member of the Board of Trustees played a role in his admission.

4.9   The distribution would drop away smoothly to the right for the same reason that it always does—there are few high-scoring people. It would drop away steeply to the left because fewer of the borderline students would be admitted (no matter how high the borderline is set).

4.11 M is called a test statistic.

4.13   The alternative hypothesis is that this student was sampled from a population of students whose mean is not equal to 650.

4.15   The word "distribution" refers to the set of values obtained for any set of observations. The phrase "sampling distribution" is reserved for the distribution of outcomes (either theoretical or empirical) of a sample statistic.

4.17 a. *Research hypothesis*—Children who attend kindergarten adjust to 1st grade faster than those who do not. *Null hypothesis*—1st-grade adjustment rates are equal for children who did and did not attend Kindergarten.

b. *Research hypothesis*—Sex education in junior high school decreases the rate of pregnancies among unmarried mothers in high school. *Null hypothesis*—The rate of pregnancies among unmarried mothers in high school is the same regardless of the presence or absence of sex education in junior high school.

4.19 Finger-tapping cutoff if $\alpha = .01$:

$$z = \frac{X - \mu}{\sigma}$$

$$-2.327 = \frac{X - 100}{20}$$

$$53.46 = X$$

z score	p
2.3200	0.9898
2.3270	0.9900
2.3300	0.9901

For α to equal .01, z must be -2.327. The cutoff score is therefore 53. The corresponding value for z when a cutoff score of 53 is applied to the curve for H_1:

$$z = \frac{X - \mu}{\sigma}$$

$$= \frac{53.46 - 80}{20}$$

$$= -1.33$$

$$z = \frac{X - \mu}{\sigma}$$

$$= \frac{53.46 - 80}{}$$

Looking $z = -1.33$ up in Appendix z, we find that .9082 of the scores fall above a score of 53.46. β is therefore 0.908.

4.21 To determine whether there is a true relationship between grades and course evaluations I would find a statistic that reflected the degree of relationship between two variables. (The students will see such a statistic (r) in Chapter 9.) I would then calculate the sampling distribution of that statistic in a situation in which there is no relationship between two variables. Finally, I would calculate the statistic for a representative set of students and classes and compare my sample value with the sampling distribution of that statistic.

4.23 a. You could draw a large sample of boys and a large sample of girls in the class and calculate the mean allowance for each group. The null hypothesis would be the hypothesis that the mean allowance, in the population, for boys is the same as for girls.

16

b. I would use a two-tailed test because I want to be able to reject the null hypothesis whether girls receive significantly more or significantly less allowance than boys.

c. I would reject the null hypothesis if the difference between the two sample means were greater than I could expect to find due to chance. Otherwise I would not reject.

d. The most important thing to do would be to have some outside corroboration for the amount of allowance reported by the children.

4.25 In the parking lot example the traditional approach to hypothesis testing would test the null hypothesis that the mean time to leave a space is the same whether someone is waiting or not. If their test failed to reject the null hypothesis they would simply fail to reject the null hypothesis, and would do so at a two-tailed level of $\alpha = .05$. Jones and Tukey on the other hand would not consider that the null hypothesis of equal population means could possibly be true. They would focus on making a conclusion about which population mean is higher. A "nonsignificant result" would only mean that they didn't have enough data to draw any conclusion. Jones and Tukey would also be likely to work with a one-tailed $\alpha = .025$, but be actually making a two-tailed test because they would not have to specify a hypothesized direction of difference.

4.27 Distribution of proportion of those seeking help who are women.

The sampling distribution of proportion of women in the sample.

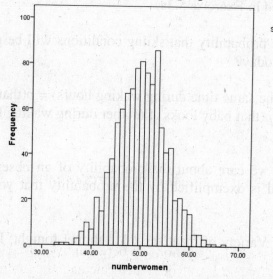

a. It is quite unlikely that we would have 61% of our sample being women if $p = .50$. In my particular sampling distribution as score of 61 or higher was obtained on 16/1000 = 1.6% of the time.

b. I would repeat the same procedure again except that I would draw from a binomial distribution where $p = .75$.

17

Chapter 5 - Basic Concepts of Probability

5.1   **a.** Analytic: If two tennis players are exactly equally skillful so that the outcome of their match is random, the probability is .50 that Player A will win the upcoming match.

      b. Relative frequency: If in past matches Player A has beaten Player B on 13 of the 17 occasions on which they played, then Player A has a probability of 13/17 = .76 of winning their upcoming match, all other things held constant.

      c. Subjective: Player A's coach feels that he has a probability of .90 of winning his upcoming match with Player B.

5.3   **a.** p(that you will win 2nd prize given that you don't win 1st) = 1/9 = .111

      b. p(that he will win 1st and you 2nd) = (2/10)(1/9) = (.20)(.111) = .022

      c. p(that you will win 1st and he 2nd) = (1/10)(2/9) = (.10)(.22) = .022

      d. p(that you are 1st and he 2nd [= .022]) + p(that he is 1st and you 2nd [= .022]) = p(that you and he will be 1st and 2nd) = .044

5.5   Conditional probabilities were involved in Exercise 5.3a.

5.7   Conditional probabilities: What is the probability that skiing conditions will be good on Wednesday, *given* that they are good today?

5.9 p(that they will look at each other at the same time during waking hours) = p(that mother looks at baby during waking hours) * p(that baby looks at mother during waking hours) = (2/13)(3/13) = (.154)(.231) = .036

5.11   A continuous distribution for which we care about the probability of an observation's falling within some specified interval is exemplified by the probability that your baby will be born on its due date.

5.13   Two examples of discrete variables: Variety of meat served at dinner tonight; Brand of desktop computer owned.

5.15   **a.** 20%, or 60 applicants, will fall at or above the 80th percentile and 10 of these will be chosen. Therefore p(that an applicant with the highest rating will be admitted) = 10/60 = .167.

      b. No one below the 80th percentile will be admitted, therefore p(that an applicant with the lowest rating will be admitted) = 0/300 = .00.

18

5.17 Mean ADDSC score for boys = 54.29, s = 12.90 [Calculated from Data Set]

a.

$$z = \frac{50 - 54.3}{12.90} = -0.33$$

Since a score of 50 is below the mean, and since we are looking for the probability of a score *greater than* 50, we want to look in the tables of the normal distribution in the column labeled "larger portion".

p(larger portion) = .6293

b. 29/55 = 53% > 50; 32/55 = 58% ≥ 50. (Notice that one percentage refers to the proportion *greater than* 50, while the other refers to the proportion *greater than or equal to* 50.)

5.19 Compare the probability of dropping out of school, ignoring the ADDSC score, with the conditional probability of dropping out given that ADDSC in elementary school exceeded some value (e.g., 66).

5.21 Plot of correct choices on trial 1 of a 5-choice task:

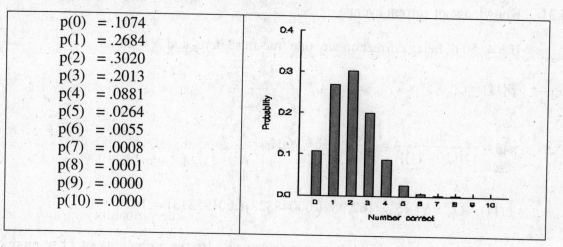

| p(0) = .1074 |
| p(1) = .2684 |
| p(2) = .3020 |
| p(3) = .2013 |
| p(4) = .0881 |
| p(5) = .0264 |
| p(6) = .0055 |
| p(7) = .0008 |
| p(8) = .0001 |
| p(9) = .0000 |
| p(10) = .0000 |

5.23 p(5 or more correct) = p(5) + p(6) + p(7) + p(8) + p(9) + p(10)

= .0264 + .0055 + .0008 + .0001 + .0000 + .0000

= .028 < .05

p(4 or more correct) = p(4) + p(5) + p(6) + p(7) + p(8) + p(9) + p(10)

= .0881 + .0264 + .0055 + .0008 + .0001 + .0000 + .0000

= .1209 > .05

At α = .05, therefore, up to 4 correct choices indicate chance performance, but 5 or more correct choices would lead me to conclude that they are no longer performing at chance levels.

5.25 If there is no housing discrimination, then a person's race and whether or not they are offered a particular unit of housing are independent events. We could calculate the probability that a particular unit (or a unit in a particular section of the city) will be offered to anyone in a specific income group. We can also calculate the probability that the customer is a member of an ethnic minority. We can then calculate the probability of that person being shown the unit assuming independence and compare that answer against the actual proportion of times a member of an ethnic minority was offered such a unit.

5.27 Number of subjects needed in Exercise 5.26's verbal learning experiment if each subject can see only two of the four classes of words:

$$P_2^4 = \frac{4!}{(4-2)!} = \frac{4!}{2!} = 12$$

5.29 The total number of ways of making ice cream cones =

$$C_6^6 + C_5^6 + C_4^6 + C_3^6 + C_2^6 + C_1^6 = 1 + 6 + 15 + 20 + 15 + 6 = 63$$

[You can't have an ice cream cone without ice cream; exclude C_0^6].

5.31 Knowledge of current events:

If $p = .50$ of being correct on any one true-false item, and $N = 20$:

$$p(11) = C_{11}^{20} \times 5^{11} \times 5^9$$

$$C_{11}^{20} = \frac{20!}{11!(20-11)!)} = \frac{20!}{11!9!} = 167,960$$

$$p(11) = C_{11}^{20} \times 5^{11} \times 5^9 = 167,960(.00048828)(.00195313) = .16$$

Since the probability of 11 correct by chance is .16, the probability of 11 <u>or more</u> correct must be greater than .16. Therefore we can not reject the hypothesis that $p = .50$ (student is guessing) at $\alpha = .05$.

5.33 Driving test passed by 22 out of 30 drivers when 60% expected to pass:

$$z = \frac{22 - 30(.60)}{\sqrt{30(.60)(.40)}} = 1.49; \text{ we cannot reject } H_0 \text{ at } \alpha = .05.$$

5.35 Students should come to understand that nature does not have a responsibility to make things come out even in the end, and that it has a terrible memory of what has happened in the past. Any "law of averages" refers to the results of a long term series of events, and it describes what we would expect to see. It does not have any self-correcting mechanism built into it.

5.37 It is low because the probability of breast cancer is itself very low. But don't be too discouraged. Having collected some data (a positive mammography) the probability is 7.8 times higher than it would otherwise have been. (And if you are a woman, please don't stop having mammographies.)

Chapter 6 - Categorical Data and Chi-Square

6.1 Popularity of psychology professors:

	Anderson	Klatsky	Kamm	Total
Observed	32	25	10	67
Expected	22.3	22.3	22.3	67

$$\chi^2 = \Sigma \frac{(O-E)^2}{E}$$

$$= \frac{(32-22.3)^2}{22.3} + \frac{(25-22.3)^2}{22.3} + \frac{(10-22.3)^2}{22.3}$$

$$= 11.33^1$$

Reject H_0 and conclude that students do not enroll at random.

6.3 Racial choice in dolls (Clark & Clark, 1939):

	Black	White	Total
Observed	83	169	252
Expected	126	126	252

$$\chi^2 = \frac{(O-E)^2}{E}$$

$$= \frac{(83-126)^2}{126} \frac{(169-126)^2}{126}$$

$$= 29.35 \quad \left[\chi^2_{.05(1)} = 3.84\right]$$

Reject H_0 and conclude that the children did not chose dolls at random (at least with respect to color). It is interesting to note that this particular study played an important role in Brown v. Board of Education (1954). In that case the U.S. Supreme Court ruled that the principle of "separate but equal", which had been the rule supporting segregation in the public schools, was no longer acceptable. Studies such as those of the Clarks had illustrated the negative effects of segregation on self-esteem and other variables.

---

[1] The answers to these questions may differ substantially, depending on the number of decimal places that are carried for the calculations.

6.7 Combining the two racial choice experiments:

Study	Black	White	Total
1939	83	169	252
	(106.42)	(145.58)	
1970	61	28	89
	(37.58)	(51.42)	
	144	197	341 = N

$$\chi^2 = \sum \frac{(O-E)^2}{E}$$

$$= \frac{(83-106.42)^2}{106.42} + \frac{(169-145.58)^2}{145.58} + \frac{(61-37.58)^2}{37.58} + \frac{(28-51.42)^2}{51.42}$$

$$= 5.154 + 3.768 + 14.595 + 10.667$$

$$= 34.184 \quad \left[\chi^2_{.05(1)} = 3.84\right]$$

Reject the H_0 and conclude that the distribution of choices between Black and White dolls was different in the two studies. Choice is *not* independent of Study. We are no longer asking whether one color of doll is preferred over the other color, but whether the *pattern* of preference is constant across studies. In analysis of variance terms we are dealing with an interaction.

6.7 **a.** Take a group of subjects at random and sort them by gender and life style (categorized three ways).

b. Deliberately take an equal number of males and females and ask them to specify a preference among 3 types of life style.

c. Deliberately take 10 males and 10 females and have them divide themselves into two teams of 10 players each.

6.9 Doubling the cell sizes:

a. $\chi^2 = 10.306$

b. This demonstrates that the obtained value of χ^2 is exactly doubled, while the critical value remains the same. Thus the sample size plays a very important role, with larger samples being more likely to produce significant results—as is also true of other tests.

23

6.11 Gender and voting behavior

	Vote		
	Yes	**No**	**Total**
Women	35	9	44
	(28.83)	(15.17)	
Men	60	41	101
	(66.17)	(34.83)	
Total	95	50	145

$$\chi^2 = \Sigma \frac{(O-E)^2}{E}$$

$$= \frac{(35-28.83)^2}{28.83} + \frac{(9-15.17)^2}{15.17} + \frac{(60-66.17)^2}{66.17} + \frac{(41-34.83)^2}{34.83}$$

$$= 5.50 \qquad [\chi^2_{.05(1)} = 3.84]$$

Reject H_0 and conclude that women voted differently from men. The odds of women supporting civil unions much greater than the odds of men supporting civil—the odds ratio is $(35/9)/(60/41) = 3.89/1.46 = 2.66$. The odds that women support civil unions were 2.66 times the odds that men did. That is a substantial difference, and likely reflects fundamental differences in attitude.

6.13 **a.** Weight preference in adolescent girls:

	Reducers	Maintainers	Gainers	Total
White	352	152	31	535
	(336.7)	(151.9)	(46.4)	
Black	47	28	24	99
	(62.3)	(28.1)	(8.6)	
	399	180	55	634 = N

$$\chi^2 = \Sigma \frac{(O-E)^2}{E}$$

$$= \frac{(352-336.7)^2}{336.7} + \frac{(152-151.9)^2}{151.9} + ... + \frac{(24-8.6)^2}{8.6}$$

$$= 37.141 \qquad [\chi^2_{.05(2)} = 5.99]$$

Adolescents girls' preferred weight varies with race.

b. The number of girls desiring to lose weight was far in excess of the number of girls who were overweight.

24

6.15 Analyzing Exercise 6.10 (Regular or Remedial English and frequency of ADD diagnosis) using the likelihood-ratio approach:

	1st	2nd	4th	2 & 4	5th	2 & 5	4 & 5	2,4,&5	Total
Rem.	22	2	1	3	2	4	3	4	41
Reg.	187	17	11	9	16	7	8	6	261
	209	19	12	12	18	11	11	10	302

$$\chi^2 = 2\left[\Sigma O_{ij} \ln\left[\frac{O_{ij}}{E_{ij}}\right]\right]$$
$$= 2 \times [22 \times \ln(22/28.374) + 2 \times \ln(2/2.579) + ... + 6 \times \ln(6/8.642)]$$
$$= 2 \times [22(-.25443) + 2(-0.25444) + ... + 6(-0.36492)]$$
$$= 12.753 \text{ on } 7 \text{ } df$$

Do not reject H_0.

6.17 Monday Night Football opinions, before and after watching:

	Pro to Con	Con to Pro	Total
Observed Frequencies	20	5	25
Expected Frequencies	12.5	12.5	25

$$\chi^2 = \Sigma \frac{(O-E)^2}{E} = \frac{(20-12.5)^2}{12.5} + \frac{(5-12.5)^2}{12.5}$$
$$= 4.5 + 4.5 = 9.0 \text{ on } 1 \text{ } df. \text{ Reject } H_0$$

b. If watching Monday Night Football really changes people's opinions (in a negative direction), then of those people who change, more should change from positive to negative than vice versa, which is what happened.

c. The analysis does not take into account all of those people who did not change. It only reflects direction of change if a person changes.

6.19 b. Row percents take entries as a percentage of row totals, while column percents take entries as percentage of column totals.

c. These are the probabilities (to 4 decimal places) of a $\chi^2 \geq \chi^2_{obt}$

d. The correlation between the two variables is approximately .25.

6.21 For data in Exercise 6.20a:

a. $\phi_c = \sqrt{26.90/22,071} = 0.0349$

b. Odds Fatal | Placebo = 18/10,845 = .00166.
Odds Fatal | Aspirin = 5/10,933 = .000453.
Odds Ratio = .00166/.000453 = 3.66
The odds that you will die from a myocardial infarction are 3.66 times higher if you do not take aspirin than if you do.

6.23 For Table 6.4 the odds ratio for a death sentence as a function of race is
$(33/251)/(33/508) = 2.017$. A person is about twice as likely to be sentenced to death if they are nonwhite than if they are white.

6.25 Dabbs and Morris (1990) study of testosterone.

		Testosterone		
		High	Normal	Total
	No	345	3614	3959
		(395.723)	(3563.277)	
Delinquency	Yes	101	402	503
		(50.277)	(452.723)	
		446	4016	$4462 = N$

$$\chi^2 = \sum \frac{(O-E)^2}{E}$$

$$= \frac{(345-395.723)^2}{395.723} + \frac{(3614-3563.277)^2}{3563.277} + \frac{(101-50.277)^2}{50.277} + \frac{(402-452.723)^2}{452.723}$$

$$= 64.08 \quad \left[\chi^2_{.05(1)} = 3.84 \right] \quad \text{Reject } H_0$$

6.27 Childhood delinquency in the Dabbs and Morris (1990) study.

a.

		Testosterone		
		High	Normal	Total
	No	366	3554	3920
		(391.824)	(3528.176)	
Delinquency	Yes	80	462	542
		(54.176)	(487.824)	
		446	4016	$4462 = N$

$$\chi^2 = \sum \frac{(O-E)^2}{E}$$

$$= \frac{(366-391.824)^2}{391.824} + \frac{(3554-3528.176)^2}{3528.176} + \frac{(80-54.176)^2}{54.176} + \frac{(462-487.824)^2}{487.824}$$

$$= 15.57 \quad \left[\chi^2_{.05(1)} = 3.84 \right] \quad \text{Reject } H_0$$

26

b. There is a significant relationship between high levels of testosterone in adult men and a history of delinquent behavior during childhood.

c. This result shows that we can tie the two variables (delinquency and testosterone) together historically.

6.29 Good touch/Bad touch

a.

		Abused		
		Yes	No	Total
Received Program	Yes	43 (56.85)	457 (443.15)	500
	No	50 (36.15)	268 (281.85)	318
		93	725	818 = N

$$\chi^2 = \Sigma \frac{(O-E)^2}{E}$$

$$= \frac{(43-56.85)^2}{56.85} + \frac{(457-443.15)^2}{443.15} + ... + \frac{(268-281.85)^2}{281.85}$$

$$= 9.79 \qquad \chi^2_{.05(1)} = 3.84 \quad \text{Reject } H_0$$

b. Odds ratio

OR = (43/457)/(50/268) = 0.094/0.186 = .505. Those who receive the program have about half the odds of subsequently suffering abuse.

6.31 Gender of parents and children.

a.

		Lost Parent Gender		
		Male	Female	Total
Child	Male	18	34	52
	Female	27	61	88
		45	95	140 = N

$\chi^2 = .232$
$(p = .630)$

b. There is no relationship between the gender of the lost parent and the gender of the child.

c. We would be unable to separate effects due to parent's gender from effects due to the child's gender. They would be completely confounded.

27

6.33   We could ask a series of similar questions, evenly split between "right" and "wrong" answers. We could then sort the replies into positive and negative categories and ask whether faculty were more likely than students to give negative responses.

6.35   I alluded to this when I referred to the meaning of kappa in the previous question. Kappa would be noticeably reduced if the scales used by husbands and wives were different, but the relationship could still be high.

6.37   Fidalgo's study of bullying in the work force.

a.   Collapsing over job categories

	Not Bullied	Bullied	Total
Male	461 (449.54)	68 (79.46)	529
Female	337 (342.46)	72 (60.54)	403
Total	792	140	932

$$\chi^2 = \Sigma\left(\frac{(O-E)^2}{E}\right)$$

$$= \frac{(461-449.54)^2}{449.54} + \frac{(68-79.46)^2}{79.46} + \frac{(337-342.46)^2}{342.46} + \frac{(72-60.54)^2}{60.54}$$

$$= 0.292 + 1.653 + 0.087 + 2.169 = 4.20$$

This chi-square is significant on 1 *df*

b.   The odds ratio is

$$OR = \frac{68/461}{72/337} = \frac{.1478}{.2136} = .70$$

The odds that a male will be bullied are about 70% those of a female being bullied.

c. & d.   Breaking the data down by job category

Using SPSS

	Chi-Squared	df	Asymp. Sig. (2-sided)
Cochran's	2.602	1	.107
Mantel-Haenszel	2.285	1	.131

Mantel-Haenszel Common Odds Ratio Estimate

Estimate			1.361
ln(Estimate)			.308
Std. Error of ln(Estimate)			.193
Asymp. Sig. (2-sided)			.111
Asymp. 95% Confidence Interval	Common Odds Ratio	Lower Bound	.931
		Upper Bound	1.988
	ln(Common Odds Ratio)	Lower Bound	-.071
		Upper Bound	.687

The Mantel-Haenszel common odds ratio estimate is asymptotically normally distributed under the common odds ratio of 1.000 assumption. So is the natural log of the estimate.

When we condition on job category there is no relationship between bullying and gender and the odds ratio drops to 1.36

e. For Males

Chi-Square Tests[b]

	Value	df	Asymp. Sig. (2-sided)
Pearson Chi-Square	6.609[a]	4	.158
Likelihood Ratio	7.273	4	.122
Linear-by-Linear Association	5.591	1	.018
N of Valid Cases	529		

a. 1 cells (10.0%) have expected count less than 5. The minimum expected count is 3.98.

b. Gender = Male

For Females

Chi-Square Tests[b]

	Value	df	Asymp. Sig. (2-sided)
Pearson Chi-Square	.510[a]	4	.973
Likelihood Ratio	.550	4	.968
Linear-by-Linear Association	.246	1	.620
N of Valid Cases	403		

a. 1 cells (10.0%) have expected count less than 5. The minimum expected count is 1.61.

b. Gender = Female

For males bullying declines as job categories increase, but this is not the case for women.

29

6.39   Appleton, French, & Vanderpump (1996) study:

There is a tendency for more younger people to smoke than older people. Because younger people generally have a longer life expectancy than older people, that would make the smokers appear as if they had a lower risk of death. What looks like a smoking effect is an age effect.

Risk Estimate

	Value	95% Confidence Interval	
		Lower	Upper
Odds Ratio for Dead (1.00 / 2.00)	1.460	1.141	1.868
For cohort Smoker = No	1.173	1.062	1.296
For cohort Smoker = Yes	.804	.693	.932
N of Valid Cases	1314		

Tests of Conditional Independence

	Chi-Squared	df	Asymp. Sig. (2-sided)
Cochran's	9.121	1	.003
Mantel-Haenszel	8.745	1	.003

Under the conditional independence assumption, Cochran's statistic is asymptotically distributed as a 1 df chi-squared distribution, only if the number of strata is fixed, while the Mantel-Haenszel statistic is always asymptotically distributed as a 1 df chi-squared distribution. Note that the continuity correction is removed from the Mantel-Haenszel statistic when the sum of the differences between the observed and the expected is 0.

30

Chapter 7 - Hypothesis Tests Applied to Means

7.1   Distribution of 100 random numbers:

DV

		Frequency	Percent	Valid Percent	Cumulative Percent
Valid	.00	7	7.0	7.0	7.0
	1.00	9	9.0	9.0	16.0
	2.00	14	14.0	14.0	30.0
	3.00	9	9.0	9.0	39.0
	4.00	16	16.0	16.0	55.0
	5.00	4	4.0	4.0	59.0
	6.00	10	10.0	10.0	69.0
	7.00	14	14.0	14.0	83.0
	8.00	13	13.0	13.0	96.0
	9.00	4	4.0	4.0	100.0
	Total	100	100.0	100.0	

mean(dv)   =   4.46
st. dev(dv) =   2.687
var(dv)   =   7.22

7.3   Does the Central Limit Theorem work?

The mean and standard deviation of the sample are 4.46 and 2.69. The mean and standard deviation are very close to the other parameters of the population from which the sample was drawn (4.5 and 2.7, respectively.) The mean of the distribution of means is 4.45, which is close to the population mean, and the standard deviation is 1.20.

Population Parameters	Predictions from Central Limit Theorem	Empirical Sampling distribution
$\mu = 4.5$	$\bar{X} = 4.5$	$\bar{X} = 4.45$
$\sigma^2 = 7.22$	$s^2 = \dfrac{\sigma^2}{n} = \dfrac{7.22}{5} = 1.44$	$s^2 = 1.44$

The mean of the sampling distribution is approximately correct compared to that predicted by the Central Limit theorem. The variance of the sampling distribution is almost exactly what we would have predicted..

7.5   The standard error would have been smaller, because it would be estimated by $\sqrt{\dfrac{7.29}{15}}$ instead of $\sqrt{\dfrac{7.29}{5}}$.

7.7   I used a two-tailed test in the last problem, but a one-tailed test could be justified on the grounds that we had no interest is showing that these students thought that they were below average, but only in showing that they thought that they were above average.

31

7.9   While the group that was near the bottom certainly had less room to underestimate their performance than to overestimate it, the fact that they overestimated by so much is significant. (If they were in the bottom quartile the best that they could have scored was at the 25th percentile, yet their mean estimate was at the 68th percentile.)

7.11   Everitt's data on weight gain:

The Mean gain = 3.01, standard deviation = 7.31. t = 2.22. With 28 df the critical value = 2.048, so we will reject the null hypothesis and conclude that the girls gained at better than chance levels. The effect size is 3.01/7.31 = 0.41.

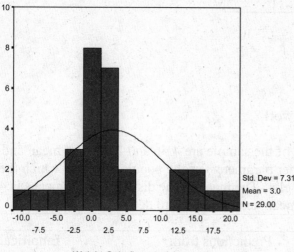

Std. Dev = 7.31
Mean = 3.0
N = 29.00

Weight Gain (in pounds)

7.13   **a.**   Performance when not reading passage

$$t = \frac{\overline{X} - \mu}{s_{\overline{X}}} = \frac{\overline{X} - \mu}{\dfrac{s}{\sqrt{n}}}$$

$$= \frac{46.6 - 20.0}{\dfrac{6.8}{\sqrt{28}}} = \frac{26.6}{1.285} = 20.70$$

   b.   This does not mean that the SAT is not a valid measure, but it does show that people who do well at guessing at answers also do well on the SAT. This is not very surprising.

32

7.15 Confidence limits on μ for Exercise 7.14:

$$CI_{.95} = \bar{X} \pm t_{.05}\frac{s}{\sqrt{n}}$$

$$= 4.39 \pm 2.03\frac{2.61}{\sqrt{36}} = 4.39 \pm 0.883$$

$$= 3.507 \le \mu \le 5.273$$

An interval formed as this one was has a probability of .95 of encompassing the mean of the population. Since this interval includes the hypothesized population mean of 3.87, it is consistent with the results in Exercise 7.14.

7.17 Confidence limits on beta-endorphin changes:

$$CI_{.95} = \bar{D} \pm t_{.05}\frac{s_D}{\sqrt{n}}$$

$$= 7.70 \pm 2.101\frac{9.945}{\sqrt{19}} = 7.70 \pm 4.794$$

$$= 2.906 \le \mu \le 12.494$$

7.19 Paired *t* test on marital satisfaction:

$$t = \frac{\bar{X}_1 - \bar{X}_2}{s_{\bar{X}_1 - \bar{X}_2}} = \frac{\bar{D}}{s_{\bar{D}}} = \frac{\bar{D}}{\dfrac{s_D}{\sqrt{n}}}$$

$$= \frac{2.725 - 2.791}{\dfrac{1.30}{\sqrt{91}}} = \frac{-.066}{.136} = -.485$$

We cannot reject the null hypothesis that males and females are equally satisfied. A paired-*t* is appropriate because it would not seem reasonable to assume that the sexual satisfaction of a husband is independent of that of his wife.

7.21 Correlation between husbands and wives:

$$r = \frac{\text{cov}_{XY}}{s_X s_Y} = \frac{0.420}{\sqrt{(1.357)(1.167)}} = \frac{0.420}{1.584} = \frac{.420}{1.259} = .334$$

The correlation between the scores of husbands and wives was .334, which is significant, and which confirms the assumption that the scores would be related.

33

7.23 The important question is what would the sampling distribution of the mean (or differences between means) look like, and with 91 pairs of scores that sampling distribution would be substantially continuous with a normal distribution of means.

7.25 Sullivan and Bybee study:

$$\bar{X}_{int} = 5.03 \quad s_{int} = 1.01 \quad n_{int} = 135$$
$$\bar{X}_{ctrl} = 4.61 \quad s_{int} = 1.13 \quad n_{int} = 130$$

$$t = \frac{\bar{X}_{int} - \bar{X}_{ctrl}}{\sqrt{\dfrac{s_{int}^2}{n_{int}} + \dfrac{s_{ctrl}^2}{n_{ctrl}}}} = \frac{5.03 - 4.61}{\sqrt{\dfrac{1.01^2}{135} + \dfrac{1.13^2}{130}}}$$

$$= \frac{5.03 - 4.61}{\sqrt{\dfrac{1.02}{135} + \dfrac{1.277}{130}}} = \frac{0.42}{\sqrt{0.027}} = \frac{0.42}{0.165} = 2.545$$

$$p(t > abs(2.545)) = .011$$

The quality of life was significantly better for the intervention group.

7.27 Paired *t*-test on before and after intervention quality of life

$$\bar{X}_{before} = 4.47 \quad \bar{X}_{after} = 5.03 \quad s_{diff} = 1.30 \quad n = 135$$

$$t = \frac{\bar{D} - 0}{\dfrac{s_{diff}}{\sqrt{n}}} = \frac{5.03 - 4.47}{\dfrac{1.30}{\sqrt{135}}} = \frac{0.56}{.006} = 93.33$$

$$p < .000$$

Confidence limits on weight gain in Cognitive Behavior Therapy group:

$$CI_{.95} = \bar{D} \pm t_{.025(28)} s_{\bar{D}}$$
$$= 3.02 \pm (2.05)(1.357) = 3.02 \pm 2.78$$
$$0.24 \le \mu \le 5.80$$

The probability is .95 that this procedure has resulted in limits that bracket the mean weight gain in the population.

7.29 Katz et al (1990) study

a. Null hypothesis—there is not a significant difference in test scores between those who have read the passage and those who have not.

b. Alternative hypothesis—there is a significant difference between the two conditions.

34

c.

$$t = \frac{\bar{X}_1 - \bar{X}_2}{\sqrt{\dfrac{s^2}{n_1} + \dfrac{s^2}{n_2}}} \qquad \text{where} \quad s^2 = \frac{(n_1 - 1)s_1^2 + (n_2 - 1)s_2^2}{n_1 + n_2 - 2}$$

$$s^2 = \frac{16(10.6^2) + 27(6.8^2)}{17 + 28 - 2} = \frac{3046.24}{43} = 70.843$$

$$t = \frac{69.6 - 46.6}{\sqrt{\dfrac{70.843}{17} + \dfrac{70.843}{28}}} = \frac{23.0}{\sqrt{70.843\left(\dfrac{1}{17} + \dfrac{1}{28}\right)}} = \frac{23.0}{\sqrt{6.697}} = 8.89$$

$t = 8.89$ on 43 df if we pool the variances. This difference is significant.

d. We can conclude that students do better on this test if they read the passage on which they are going to answer questions.

7.31

$$t = \frac{\bar{X}_1 - \bar{X}_2}{\sqrt{\dfrac{s^2}{n_1} + \dfrac{s^2}{n_2}}} \qquad \text{where} \quad s^2 = \frac{(n_1 - 1)s_1^2 + (n_2 - 1)s_2^2}{n_1 + n_2 - 2}$$

$$s^2 = \frac{25(63.82) + 28(53.41)}{26 + 29 - 2} = \frac{3090.98}{53} = 58.32$$

$$t = \frac{-0.45 - 3.01}{\sqrt{\dfrac{58.32}{26} + \dfrac{58.32}{29}}} = \frac{-3.46}{\sqrt{58.32\left(\dfrac{1}{26} + \dfrac{1}{29}\right)}} = \frac{-3.46}{\sqrt{4.254}} = \frac{--3.46}{2.062} = -1.68$$

A t on two independent groups $= -1.68$ on 53 df, which is not significant. Cognitive behavior therapy did not lead to significantly greater weight gain than the Control condition. (Variances were homogeneous.)

7.33 If those means had actually come from independent samples, we could not remove differences due to couples, and the resulting t would have been somewhat smaller.

7.35 The difference between the two answers in not greater than it is because the correlation between husbands and wives was actually quite low.

7.37 **a.** I would assume that the experimental hypothesis is the hypothesis that mothers of schizophrenic children provide TAT descriptions that show less positive parent-child relationships.

b. Normal   Mean = 3.55 $s = 1.887$ $n = 20$
     Schizophrenic   Mean = 2.10 $s = 1.553$ $n = 20$

$$t = \frac{\bar{X}_1 - \bar{X}_2}{\sqrt{\dfrac{s_1^2}{n_1} + \dfrac{s_2^2}{n_2}}} = \frac{3.55 - 2.10}{\sqrt{\dfrac{1.887^2}{20} + \dfrac{1.553^2}{20}}}$$

$$= \frac{1.45}{\sqrt{0.299}} = \frac{1.45}{0.546} = 2.66$$

$[t_{.05}(38) = \pm 2.02]$ Reject the null hypothesis

This t is significant on 38 df, and I would conclude that the mean number of pictures portraying positive parent-child relationships is lower in the schizophrenic group than in the normal group.

7.39 There is no way to tell cause and effect relationships in Exercise 7.37. It could be that people who experience poor parent-child interaction are at risk for schizophrenia. But it could also be that schizophrenic children disrupt the family and poor relationships come as a result.

7.41 95% confidence limits:

$$CI_{.05} = \left(\bar{X}_1 - \bar{X}_2 \right) \pm t_{.025} \sqrt{\frac{s^2}{n_1} + \frac{s^2}{n_2}}$$

$$= (18.778 - 17.625) \pm (2.131)\sqrt{\frac{16.362}{9} + \frac{16.362}{8}} = 1.153 \pm 4.189$$

$$-3.036 \leq (\mu_1 - \mu_2) \leq 5.342$$

7.43   Repeating Exercise 7.42 with time as the dependent variable:

$$t = \frac{\bar{X}_1 - \bar{X}_2}{\sqrt{\dfrac{s_1^2}{n_1} + \dfrac{s_2^2}{n_2}}}$$

$$t = \frac{2.102 - 1.246}{\sqrt{\dfrac{0.714}{5} + \dfrac{0.091}{5}}} = \frac{0.856}{\sqrt{0.161}} = \frac{0.856}{0.401} = 2.134$$

The variances are very different, but even if we did not adjust the degrees of freedom, we would still fail to reject the null hypothesis.

7.45   If you take the absolute differences between the observations and their group means and run a t test comparing the two groups on the absolute differences, you obtain $t = 0.625$. Squaring this you have $F = 0.391$, which makes it clear that Levene's test in SPSS is operating on the absolute differences. (The t for squared differences would equal 0.213, which would give an F of 0.045.)

7.47   Differences between males and females on anxiety and depression:

(We cannot assume homogeneity of regression here.)

Independent Samples Test

Equal variances not assumed

| | t-test for Equality of Means | | | | | | |
| | | | | | | 95% Confidence Interval of the Difference | |
	t	df	Sig. (2-tailed)	Mean Difference	Std. Error Difference	Lower	Upper
DEPRESST	3.256	248.346	.001	3.426	1.052	1.353	5.499
ANXT	1.670	246.260	.096	1.805	1.081	-.324	3.933

7.49   Effect size for data in Exercise 7.25:

$$d = \frac{\bar{X}_{After} - \bar{X}_{Before}}{s_{Before}} = \frac{3.02}{4.85} = 0.62$$

I chose to use the standard deviation of the before therapy scores because it provides a reasonable base against which to standardize the mean difference. The confidence intervals on the difference, which is another way to examine the size of an effect, were given in the answer to Exercise 7.27.

7.51 **a.** The scale of measurement is important because if we rescaled the categories as 1, 2, 4, and 6, for example, we would have quite different answers.

b. The first exercise asks if there is a relationship between the satisfaction of husbands and wives. The second simply asks if males (husbands) are more satisfied, on average, than females (wives).

c. You could adapt the suggestion made in the text about combining the *t* on independent groups and the *t* on matched groups.

d. I'm really not very comfortable with the *t* test because I am not pleased with the scale of measurement. An alternative would be a ranked test, but the number of ties is huge, and that probably worries me even more.

Chapter 8 - Power

8.1 Peer pressure study:

a.

$$d = \frac{\mu_1 - \mu_0}{\sigma}$$
$$= \frac{520 - 500}{80}$$
$$= .25$$

b. $f(n)$ for 1-sample t-test $= \sqrt{n}$

$$\delta = d\sqrt{n}$$
$$= .25\sqrt{100}$$
$$= 2.5$$

c. Power $= .71$

8.3 Changing power in Exercise 8.1:

a. For power $= .70$, $\delta = 2.475$

$$\delta = d\sqrt{n}$$
$$2.475 = .25\sqrt{n}$$
$$n = 98.01 \approx 99 \text{ (Round up, because students come in whole lots)}$$

b. For power $= .80$, $\delta = 2.8$

$$\delta = d\sqrt{n}$$
$$2.8 = .25\sqrt{n}$$
$$n = 125.44 \approx 126 \text{ (Round up)}$$

c. For power $= .90$, $\delta = 3.25$

$$\delta = d\sqrt{n}$$
$$3.25 = .25\sqrt{n}$$
$$n = 169$$

8.5 Sampling distributions of the mean for the situation in Exercise 8.4:

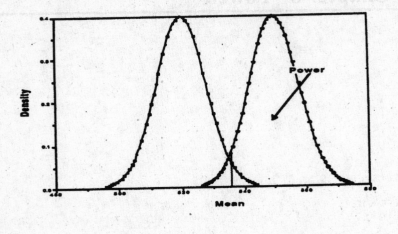

8.7 Avoidance behavior in rabbits using 1-sample t test:

a.

$$d = \frac{\mu_1 - \mu_0}{\sigma} = \frac{5.8 - 4.8}{2} = \frac{1}{2} = .50$$

For power = .50, $\delta = 1.95$

$$\delta = d\sqrt{n}$$
$$1.95 = .5\sqrt{n}$$
$$n = 15.21 \approx 16$$

b. For power = .80, $\delta = 2.8$
$$\delta = d\sqrt{n}$$
$$2.8 = .5\sqrt{n}$$
$$n = 31.36 \approx 32$$

8.9 Avoidance behavior in rabbits with unequal Ns:

$$d = .5$$
$$n = \bar{n}_\text{h} = \frac{2n_1 n_2}{n_1 + n_2}$$
$$= \frac{2(20)(15)}{20 + 15} = 17.14$$
$$\delta = d\sqrt{\frac{n}{2}} = .5\sqrt{\frac{17.14}{2}} = 1.46$$

power = .31

8.11 *t* test on data for Exercise 8.10

$$t = \frac{\bar{X}_1 - \bar{X}_2}{\sqrt{\dfrac{s_p^2}{n_1} + \dfrac{s_p^2}{n_2}}}$$

$$= \frac{25 - 30}{\sqrt{\dfrac{64}{20} + \dfrac{64}{20}}}$$

$$= -1.98$$

$[t_{.025}(38) = \pm 2.025]$ Do not reject the null hypothesis

c. *t* is numerically equal to δ although *t* is calculated from statistics and δ is calculated from parameters. In other words, δ = the *t* that you would get if the data exactly match what you think are the values of the parameters.

8.13 Diagram to defend answer to Exercise 8.12:

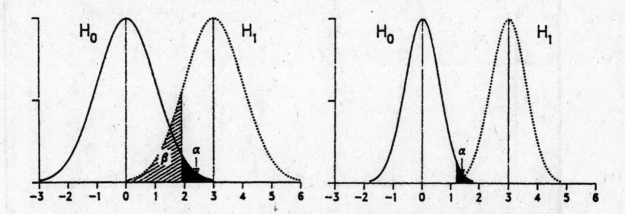

With larger sample sizes the sampling distribution of the mean has a smaller standard error, which means that there is less overlap of the distributions. This results in greater power, and therefore the larger *n*'s significant result was less impressive.

8.15 Social awareness of ex-delinquents--which subject pool would be better to use?

$$\bar{X}_{normal} = 38 \qquad n = 50$$

$$\bar{X}_{H.S.\ Grads} = 35 \quad n = 100$$

$$\bar{X}_{dropout} = 30 \qquad n = 25$$

41

$$d = \frac{38-35}{\sigma}$$

$$\overline{n}_h = \frac{2(50)(100)}{150} = 66.67$$

$$\delta = \frac{3}{\sigma}\sqrt{\frac{66.67}{2}} = \frac{17.32}{\sigma}$$

$$d = \frac{38-30}{\sigma}$$

$$\overline{n}_h = \frac{2(50)(25)}{75} = 33.33$$

$$\delta = \frac{8}{\sigma}\sqrt{\frac{33.33}{2}} = \frac{32.66}{\sigma}$$

Assuming equal standard deviations, the H.S. dropout group of 25 would result in a higher value of δ and therefore higher power. (You can let σ be any value you choose, as long as it is the same for both calculations. Then calculate δ for each situation.)

8.17 Stereotyped threat in women

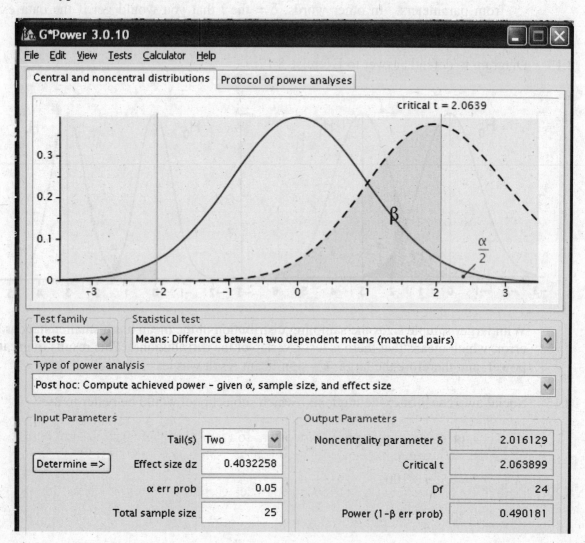

Here the power is about one half of what it was in the study using men, reflecting the fact that our group of men had a stronger identification with their skills in math.

8.19 When can power = β?

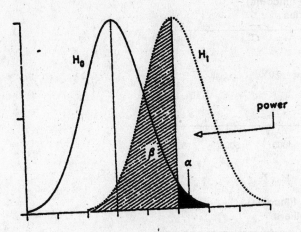

The mean under H_1 should fall at the critical value under H_0. The question implies a one-tailed test. Thus the mean is 1.645 standard errors above μ_0, which is 100.

$$\mu = 100 + 1.64\sigma_X$$
$$= 100 + 1.645\left(15/\sqrt{25}\right)$$
$$= 104.935$$

When μ = 104.935, power would equal β.

8.21 Aronson's study:
   a. The study would confound differences in lab that have nothing to do with the independent variable with the effect of that variable. You would not be able to draw sound conclusions unless you could persuade yourself that the labs were similar in all other relevant ways.

   b. I would randomize the conditions across all of the students in the two labs combined.

   c. The stereotypes do not apply to women, so I don't have any particular hypothesis about what would happen.

8.23 Both of these questions point to the need to design studies carefully so that the results are clear and interpretable.

43

Chapter 9 - Correlation and Regression

9.1 Infant Mortality in Sub-Saharan Africa
a. & b.

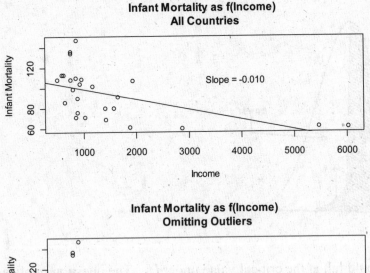

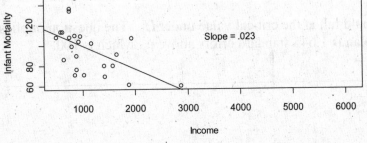

c. Those two points would almost certainly draw the line toward them, which will flatten the slope. If we remove those countries we have the second graph with a steeper slope.

9.3 Significance of correlations

The minimum sample size in this example is 25, and we will use that. We would need $t = 2.069$ for a two-tailed test on $N - 2 = 23$ *df*. A little (well, maybe a lot) of algebra will show that a correlation of .396 will produce that *t* value.

9.5 If we put these two predictors together using methods covered in Chapter 15, the multiple correlation will be .58, which is only a small amount higher than Income alone.

9.7 I suspect that a major reason why this variable does not play a more important role is the fact that it has very little variance. The range is 3% - 7%. One cause of this may be the very high death rate among women in sub-saharan Africa. There are many fewer women giving birth at ages above 40. To quote from a United Nations report (http://www.un.org/ecosocdev/geninfo/women/women96.htm):

44

- Women are becoming increasingly affected by HIV. Today about 42 per cent of estimated cases are women, and the number of infected women is expected to reach 15 million by the year 2000.

- An estimated 20 million unsafe abortions are performed worldwide every year, resulting in the deaths of 70,000 women.

- Approximately 585,000 women die every year, over 1,600 every day, from causes related to pregnancy and childbirth. In sub-Saharan Africa, 1 in 13 women will die from pregnancy or childbirth related causes, compared to 1 in 3,300 women in the United States.

- Globally, 43 per cent of all women and 51 per cent of pregnant women suffer from iron-deficiency anemia.

9.9 Psychologists are very much interested in studying variables related to behavior and in finding ways to change behavior. I would guess that they would have a good deal to say about educating women in ways that would decrease infant mortality.

9.11 The relationship is decidedly curvilinear, and Pearson's r is a statistic on linear relationships.

9.13 Power for $n = 25$, $\rho = .20$

$$d = \rho_1 = .20$$
$$\delta = \rho_1 \sqrt{N-1} = .20\sqrt{24} = 0.98$$
$$\text{power} \approx .17$$

9.15 Number of symptoms predicted for a stress score of 8 using the data in Table 9.2 :

Regression equation: $\hat{Y} = 0.0086(X) + 4.30$

If Stress score $(X) = 8$: $\hat{Y} = 0.0086(8) + 4.30$

Predicted ln(symptoms) score is : $\hat{Y} = 4.37$

9.17 Confidence interval on $\hat{Y}$:

I will calculate them for X incrementing between 0 and 60 in steps of 10

45

$$CI(Y) = \hat{Y} \pm t_{\alpha/2}\left(s'_{Y.X}\right)$$

$$s'_{Y.X} = s_{Y.X}\sqrt{1 + \frac{1}{N} + \frac{(X_i - \bar{X})^2}{(N-1)s_X^2}} = 0.1726\sqrt{1 + \frac{1}{107} + \frac{(X_i - \bar{X})^2}{106(156.05)}}$$

$$\hat{Y} = 0.00856X + 4.30$$

$$t_{\alpha/2} = 1.983$$

For X from 0 to 60 in steps of 10, s'$_{Y.X}$=
0.1757 0.1741 0.1734 0.1738 0.1752 0.1776 0.1810

$$CI(Y) = \hat{Y} \pm (t_{\alpha/2})(s'_{Y.X})$$

For several different values of X, calculate $\hat{Y}$ and s'$_{Y.X}$ and plot the results.

X =	0	10	20	30	40	50	60
$\hat{Y}$ =	4.300	4.386	4.471	4.557	4.642	4.728	4.814

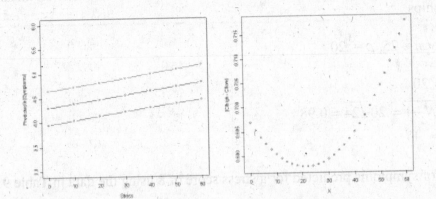

The curvature is hard to see, but it is there, as can be seen in the graphic on the right, which plots the width of the interval as a function of X. (It's fun to play with R).

9.19   Galton's data

a.

Coefficients[a]

Model		Unstandardized Coefficients		Standardized Coefficients	t	Sig.
		B	Std. Error	Beta		
1	(Constant)	23.942	2.811		8.517	.000
	midparent	.646	.041	.459	15.711	.000

46

Coefficients[a]

Model		Unstandardized Coefficients		Standardized Coefficients	t	Sig.
		B	Std. Error	Beta		
1	(Constant)	23.942	2.811		8.517	.000
	midparent	.646	.041	.459	15.711	.000

a. Dependent Variable: child

b. Predicted height = 0.646*(Midparent) + 23.942

c. Child Means

Descriptives

child

	N	Mean	Std. Deviation	Std. Error	95% Confidence Interval for Mean	
					Lower Bound	Upper Bound
1	392	67.12	2.247	.113	66.90	67.35
2	219	68.02	2.240	.151	67.72	68.32
3	183	68.71	2.465	.182	68.35	69.06
4	134	70.18	2.269	.196	69.79	70.57
Total	928	68.09	2.518	.083	67.93	68.25

Parent means

Descriptives

midparent

	N	Mean	Std. Deviation	Std. Error	95% Confidence Interval for Mean	
					Lower Bound	Upper Bound
1	392	66.66	1.068	.054	66.56	66.77
2	219	68.50	.000	.000	68.50	68.50
3	183	69.50	.000	.000	69.50	69.50
4	134	71.18	.786	.068	71.04	71.31
Total	928	68.31	1.787	.059	68.19	68.42

47

d. Parents in the highest quartile have a mean of 71.18, while their children have a mean of 70.18. Those parents in the lowest quartile have a mean of 66.66, while their children have a mean of 67.14. This is what we would expect to happen.

e.

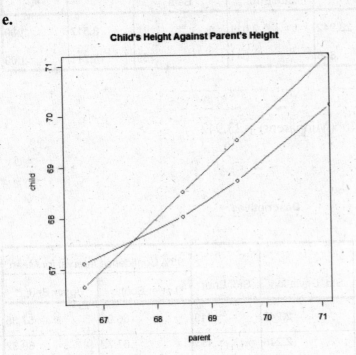

Child's Height Against Parent's Height

9.21 Number of subjects needed in Exercise 9.20 for power = .80:

For power = .80, $\delta = 2.80$

$$\delta = \rho_1 \sqrt{N-1}$$
$$2.80 = .40\sqrt{N-1}$$
$$\sqrt{N-1} = 2.80 / .40 = 7$$
$$N = 50$$

9.23 Katz et al. correlations with SAT scores.

a. $r_1 = .68$ $r_1' = .829$
$r_2 = .51$ $r_2' = .563$

$$z = \frac{r_1' - r_2'}{\sqrt{\dfrac{1}{N_1 - 3} + \dfrac{1}{N_2 - 3}}} = \frac{.829 - .563}{\sqrt{\dfrac{1}{14} + \dfrac{1}{25}}}$$

$= 0.797$

The correlations are not significantly different from each other.

48

b. We do not have reason to argue that the relationship between performance and prior test scores is affected by whether or not the student read the passage.

9.25 It is difficult to tell whether the significant difference between the results of the two previous problems is to be attributable to the larger sample sizes or the higher (and thus more different) values of r'. It is likely to be the former.

9.27 Moore and McCabe example of alcohol and tobacco use:

Correlations

		ALCOHOL	TOBACCO
ALCOHOL	Pearson Correlation	1.000	.224
	Sig. (2-tailed)	.	.509
	N	11	11
TOBACCO	Pearson Correlation	.224	1.000
	Sig. (2-tailed)	.509	.
	N	11	11

b. The data suggest that people from Northern Ireland actually drink relatively little.

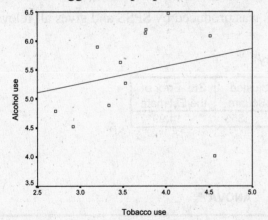

c. With Northern Ireland excluded from the data the correlation is .784, which is significant at $p = .007$.

9.29 **a.** The correlations range between .40 and .80.

b. The subscales are not measuring independent aspects of psychological well-being.

9.31   Relationship between height and weight for males:

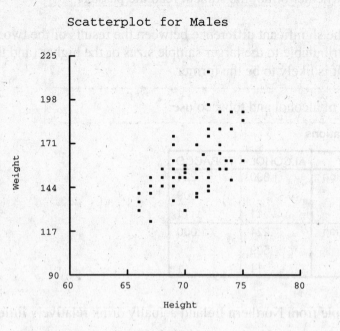

Scatterplot for Males

The regression solution that follows was produced by SPSS and gives all relevant results.

Model Summary[b]

Model	R	R Square	Adjusted R Square	Std. Error of the Estimate
1	.604[a]	.364	.353	14.9917

a. Predictors: (Constant), HEIGHT

b. Gender = Male

ANOVA[b,c]

Model		Sum of Squares	df	Mean Square	F	Sig.
1	Regression	7087.800	1	7087.800	31.536	.000[a]
	Residual	12361.253	55	224.750		
	Total	19449.053	56			

a. Predictors: (Constant), HEIGHT

b. Dependent Variable: WEIGHT

c. Gender = Male

Coefficients^{a,b}

Model		Unstandardized Coefficients		Standardized Coefficients	t	Sig.
		B	Std. Error	Beta		
1	(Constant)	-149.934	54.917		-2.730	.008
	HEIGHT	4.356	.776	.604	5.616	.000

a. Dependent Variable: WEIGHT

b. Gender = Male

With a slope of 4.36, the data predict that two males who differ by one inch will also differ by approximately 4 1/3 pounds. The intercept has no meaning because people are not 0 inches tall, but the fact that it is so largely negative suggests that there is some curvilinearity in this relationship for low values of Height.

Tests on the correlation and the slope are equivalent tests when we have one predictor, and these tests tell us that both are significant. Weight increases reliably with increases in height.

9.33   As a 5'8" male, my predicted weight is $\hat{Y}$ = 4.356(Height) - 149.934 = 4.356*68 - 149.934 = 146.27 pounds.

a. I weigh 146 pounds. (Well, I did two years ago.) Therefore the residual in the prediction is $Y - \hat{Y}$ = 146 - 146.27 = -0.27.

b. If the students on which this equation is based under- or over-estimated their own height or weight, the prediction for my weight will be based on invalid data and will be systematically in error.

9.35   The male would be predicted to weigh 137.562 pounds, while the female would be predicted to weigh 125.354 pounds. The predicted difference between them would be 12.712 pounds.

9.37   Independence of trials in reaction time study.

The data were plotted by "trial", where a larger trial number represents an observation later in the sequence.

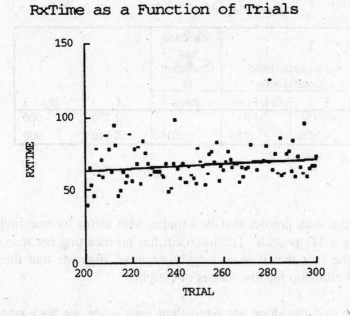

RxTime as a Function of Trials

Although the regression line has a slight positive slope, the slope is not significantly different from zero. This is shown below.

```
DEP VAR:  TRIAL      N:      100  MULTIPLE R: 0.181   SQUARED MULTIPLE R: 0.033
ADJUSTED SQUARED MULTIPLE R: 0.023     STANDARD ERROR OF ESTIMATE:     28.67506


VARIABLE      COEFFICIENT    STD ERROR    STD COEF TOLERANCE    T  P(2 TAIL)

CONSTANT      221.84259     15.94843      0.00000     .       .14E+02  .10E-14
RXTIME          0.42862      0.23465      0.18146  1.00000  1.82665  0.07080


                    ANALYSIS OF VARIANCE
SOURCE      SUM-OF-SQUARES  DF  MEAN-SQUARE     F-RATIO      P

REGRESSION    2743.58452     1  2743.58452     3.33664    0.07080
RESIDUAL     80581.41548    98   822.25934
```

There is not a systematic linear or cyclical trend over time, and we would probably be safe in assuming that the observations can be treated as if they were independent. Any slight dependency would not alter our results to a meaningful degree.

9.39   What about Eris?

Eris doesn't fit the plot as well as I would have liked. It is a bit too far away.

52

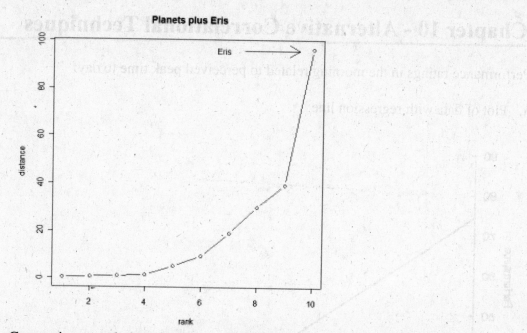

9.41 Comparing correlations in males and females.

$$z = \frac{r_1' - r_2'}{\sqrt{\dfrac{1}{N_1 - 3} + \dfrac{1}{N_2 - 3}}}$$

$$= \frac{.648 - .343}{\sqrt{\dfrac{1}{284} + \dfrac{1}{222}}} = \frac{.305}{\sqrt{0.0085}} = \frac{.305}{.092}$$

$$= 3.30$$

The difference between the two correlations is significant.

Chapter 10 - Alternative Correlational Techniques

10.1   Performance ratings in the morning related to perceived peak time to day:

a. Plot of data with regression line:

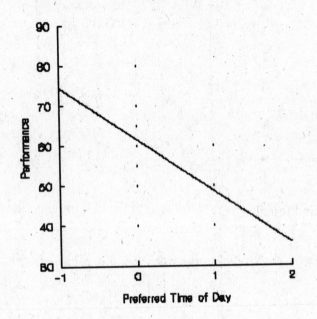

b.

$$s_X = 0.489$$

$$s_Y = 11.743$$

$$cov_{XY} = -3.105$$

$$r_{pb} = \frac{cov_{XY}}{s_X s_Y} = \frac{-3.105}{(0.489)(11.743)} = -.540$$

$$t = \frac{r\sqrt{(N-2)}}{\sqrt{1-r^2}} = \frac{(-.540)\sqrt{18}}{\sqrt{.708}} = \frac{-2.291}{.842} = -2.723 \quad [p < .01]$$

c. Performance in the morning is significantly related to people's perceptions of their peak periods.

10.3   It looks as if morning people vary their performance across time, but that evening people are uniformly poor.

10.5   Running a t test on the data in Exercise 10.1:

$$\overline{X}_1 = 61.538 \qquad s_1^2 = 114.103 \qquad n_1 = 13$$

$$\overline{X}_2 = 48.571 \qquad s_2^2 = 80.952 \qquad n_2 = 7$$

$$s_p^2 = \frac{(n_1-1)s_1^2 + (n_2-1)s_2^2}{n_1+n_2-2} = \frac{(13-1)114.103 + (7-1)80.952}{13+7-2} = 103.053$$

$$t = \frac{\overline{X}_1 - \overline{X}_2}{\sqrt{s_p^2\left(\dfrac{1}{n_1}+\dfrac{1}{n_2}\right)}} = \frac{61.538-48.571}{\sqrt{103.053\left(\dfrac{1}{13}+\dfrac{1}{7}\right)}} = 2.725$$

$$[t_{.025(18)} = \pm 2.101] \qquad\qquad \text{Reject } H_0$$

The t calculated here (2.725) is equal to the t calculated to test the significance of the r calculated in Exercise 10.1.

10.7   Regression equation for relationship between college GPA and completion of Ph.D. program:

$$b = \frac{\mathrm{cov}_{XY}}{s_X^2} = \frac{0.051}{.503^2} = .202$$

$$a = \frac{\Sigma Y - b\Sigma X}{N} = \frac{17 - .202(72.58)}{25} = .093$$

$$\hat{Y} = bX + a = .202X + .093$$

When $X = \overline{X} = 2.9032$, $\hat{Y} = .202(2.9032) + .093 = .680 = \overline{Y}$.

10.9   Establishment of a GPA cutoff of 3.00:

a.

Ph.D. (Y):	0	0	0	0	0	0	0	0	1	1
	1	1	1	1	1	1	1	1	1	1	1	1
	1	1	1							

GPA (X):	0	1	0	1	1	0	0	0	1	0
	1	1	1	1	0	1	1	1	0	0	0	1
	1	1	0							

b.

$$s_X = 0.507$$

$$s_Y = 0.476$$

$$cov_{XY} = 0.062$$

$$\phi = \frac{0.062}{(0.507)(0.476)} = .256$$

c.

$$t = \frac{r\sqrt{(N-2)}}{\sqrt{1-r^2}} = \frac{(.256)\sqrt{23}}{\sqrt{.934}} = \frac{1.228}{.967} = 1.27 \quad \text{[not significant]}$$

10.11 Alcoholism and childhood history of ADD:

a.

$$s_X = 0.471$$

$$s_Y = 0.457$$

$$cov_{XY} = 0.135$$

$$\phi = \frac{0.135}{(0.471)(0.457)} = .628$$

b. $\chi^2 = N\phi^2 = 32(.628^2) = 12.62 \ [p < .05]$

10.13 Development ordering of language skills using Kendall's τ

a.
$$\tau = 1 - \frac{2(\text{\# inversions})}{\text{\# pairs}} = 1 - \frac{2(6)}{15(14)/2} = 1 - \frac{23}{105} = .886$$

b.
$$z = \frac{\tau}{\sqrt{\dfrac{2(2N+5)}{9N(N-1)}}} = \frac{.886}{\sqrt{\dfrac{2(30+5)}{9(15)(14)}}} = \frac{.886}{\sqrt{.037}} = 4.60 \quad [p < .05]$$

10.15 Ranking of videotapes of children's behaviors by clinical graduate students and experienced clinicians using Kendall's τ:

Experienced	New	Inversions
1	2	1
2	1	0
3	4	1
4	3	0
5	5	0
6	8	2

Experienced	New	Inversions
7	6	0
8	10	2
9	7	0
10	9	0

$$\tau = 1 - \frac{2(\# \text{ inversions})}{\# \text{ pairs}} = 1 = \frac{2(6)}{10(9)/2} = 1 - \frac{12}{45} = .733$$

10.17 Verification of Rosenthal and Rubin's statement

	Improvement	No Improvement	Total
Therapy	66	34	100
	(50)	(50)	
No Therapy	34	66	100
	(50)	(50)	
Total	100	100	200

a.

$$\chi^2 = \Sigma \frac{(O-E)^2}{E} = \frac{(66-50)^2}{50} + \frac{(34-50)^2}{50} + \frac{(34-50)^2}{50} + \frac{(66-50)^2}{50}$$

$$= 20.48$$

b. An $r^2 = .0512$ would correspond to $\chi^2 = 10.24$. The closest you can come to this result is if the subjects were split 61/39 in the first condition and 39/61 in the second (rounding to integers.)

10.19 ClinCase against Group in Mireault's data

	ClinCase	
	0	1
Loss	69	66
Married	108	73
Divorced	36	23

a. $\chi^2 = 2.815$ $\qquad$ $[p = .245]$
$\phi_c = .087$

c. This approach would be preferred over the approach used in Chapter 7 if you had reason to believe that differences in depression scores below the clinical cutoff were of no importance and should be ignored.

10.21 Small Effects:

a. If a statistic is not significant, that means that we have no reason to believe that it is reliably different from 0 (or whatever the parameter under H_0). In the case of a correlation, if it is not significant, that means that we have no reason to believe that there is a relationship between the two variables. Therefore it cannot be important.

b. With the exceptions of issues of power, sample size will not make an effect more important than it is. Increasing N will increase our level of significance, but the magnitude of the effect will be unaffected.

Chapter 11 - Simple Analysis of Variance

11.1 Eysenck's study:

	Counting	Rhyming	Adjective	Imagery	Intentional	Total
Mean	7.00	6.90	11.00	13.40	12.00	10.06
St. Dev.	1.83	2.13	2.49	4.50	3.74	4.01
Variance	3.33	4.54	6.22	20.27	14.00	16.058

$$SS_{total} = \Sigma\left(X_{ij} - \bar{X}_{..}\right)^2 = (9-10.06)^2 + (8-10.06)^2 + ... + (11-10.06)^2$$
$$= 786.82$$

$$SS_{treat} = n\Sigma\left(\bar{X}_j - \bar{X}_{..}\right)^2 = 10\left((7-10.06)^2 + (6.90-10.06)^2 + ... + (12-10.06)^2\right)$$
$$= 10(35.152) = 351.52$$

$$SS_{error} = SS_{total} - SS_{treat} = 786.82 - 351.52 = 435.30$$

Summary Table

Source	df	SS	MS	F
Treatments	4	351.52	87.88	9.08
Error	45	435.30	9.67	
Total	49	786.82		

11.3 Recall in Eysenck (1974) for four Age/Levels of Processing groups:

Descriptives

RECALL

	N	Mean	Std. Deviation	Std. Error
1.00	10	6.5000	1.4337	.4534
2.00	10	19.3000	2.6687	.8439
3.00	10	7.0000	1.8257	.5774
4.00	10	12.0000	3.7417	1.1832
Total	40	11.2000	5.7699	.9123

a.

$$SS_{total} = \Sigma\left(X_{ij} - \bar{X}_{..}\right)^2 = (8-11.2)^2 + (6-11.2)^2 + ... + (11-11.2)^2$$
$$= 1298.4$$

$$SS_{treat} = n\Sigma\left(\bar{X}_j - \bar{X}_{..}\right)^2 = 10\left(\begin{array}{c}(6.5-11.2)^2 + (19.3-11.2)^2 + \\ (7.0-11.2)^2 + (12.0-11.2)^2\end{array}\right)$$
$$= 10(105.98) = 1059.8$$

$$SS_{error} = SS_{total} - SS_{treat} = 1298.4 - 1059.8 = 238.6$$

ANOVA

RECALL

	Sum of Squares	df	Mean Square	F	Sig.
Between Groups	1059.800	3	353.267	53.301	.000
Within Groups	238.600	36	6.628		
Total	1298.400	39			

b. Groups 1 and 3 combined versus 2 and 4 combined:

Descriptives

RECALL

	N	Mean	Std. Deviation	Std. Error
Low	20	6.7500	1.6182	.3618
High	20	15.6500	4.9019	1.0961
Total	40	11.2000	5.7699	.9123

$$SS_{total} = \Sigma\left(X_{ij} - \bar{X}_{..}\right)^2 = (8-11.20)^2 + (6-11.20)^2 + ... + (11-11.20)^2$$
$$= 1298.40$$

$$SS_{treat} = n\Sigma\left(\bar{X}_j - \bar{X}_{..}\right)^2 = 20\left((6.75-11.20)^2 + (15.65-11.20)^2\right)$$
$$= 20(39.605) = 792.1$$

$$SS_{error} = SS_{total} - SS_{treat} = 1298.4 - 792.1 = 502.3$$

60

ANOVA

RECALL

	Sum of Squares	df	Mean Square	F	Sig.
Between Groups	792.100	1	792.100	59.451	.000
Within Groups	506.300	38	13.324		
Total	1298.400	39			

c. The results are somewhat difficult to interpret because the error term now includes variance between younger and older participants. Notice that this is roughly double what it was in part a. In addition, we do not know whether the level of processing effect is true for both age groups, or if it applies primarily to one group

11.5 Rerun of Exercise 11.2 with additional subjects:

The following is abbreviated printout from SPSS

a.

Descriptives [a]

RECALL

	N	Mean	Std. Deviation	Std. Error
Younger	12	18.4167	3.2039	.9249
Older	10	12.0000	3.7417	1.1832
Total	22	15.5000	4.6980	1.0016

[a]. PROCESS = High

ANOVA[a]

RECALL

	Sum of Squares	df	Mean Square	F	Sig.
Between Groups	224.583	1	224.583	18.800	.000
Within Groups	238.917	20	11.946		
Total	463.500	21			

[a]. PROCESS = High

61

b. & c. With and without pooling variances:

Independent Samples Test [a]

		t	df	Sig. (2-tailed)	Mean Difference	Std. Error Difference
				t-test for Equality of Means		
RECALL	Equal variances assumed	4.336	20	.000	6.4167	1.4799
	Equal variances not assumed	4.273	17.893	.000	6.4167	1.5018

a. PROCESS = High

d. The squared t for the pooled case $= 4.3359^2 = 18.80$, which is the F in the analysis of variance.

11.7 Magnitude of effect measures for Exercise 11.3a:

$$\eta^2 = \frac{SS_{group}}{SS_{total}} = \frac{1059.8}{1298.4} = .82$$

$$\omega^2 = \frac{SS_{group} - (k-1)MS_{error}}{SS_{total} + MS_{error}} = \frac{1059.8 - (4-1)6.63}{1298.4 + 6.63} = .80$$

11.9 Magnitude of effect for Foa et al. (1991) study:

$$\eta^2 = \frac{SS_{group}}{SS_{total}} = \frac{507.840}{2786.907} = .18$$

$$\omega^2 = \frac{SS_{group} - (k-1)MS_{error}}{SS_{total} + MS_{error}} = \frac{507.840 - (4-1)55.587}{2786.907 + 55.587} = .12$$

11.11 Giancola study with transformed data.

Because some of the values were negative, I added 3.0 to each observation. The results below are still significant, but the F is smaller. The following boxplot shows the effect of the transformation.

ANOVA

Indv

	Sum of Squares	df	Mean Square	F	Sig.
Between Groups	4.280	4	1.070	4.117	.005
Within Groups	14.294	55	.260		
Total	18.574	59			

62

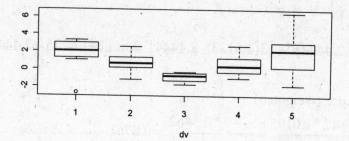

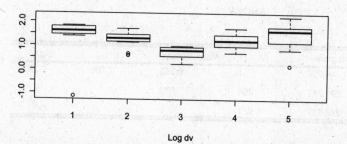

11.13 Model for Exercise 11.1:

$$X_{ij} = \mu + \tau_i = e_{ij}$$

where

μ = grand mean

τ_j = the effect of the jth treatment

e_{ij} = the unit of error for the ith subject in treatment$_j$

11.15 Model for Exercise 11.3:

$$X_{ij} = \mu + \tau_i = e_{ij}$$

where

μ = grand mean

τ_j = the effect of the jth treatment (where a "treatment" is a particular combination of Age and Task.

e_{ij} = the unit of error for the ith subject in treatment j

11.17 Howell & Huessy (1981) study of ADD in elementary school vs. GPA in high school:

Group	Group Means	s_j^2	n_j
Never ADD	2.6774	0.9450	201
2nd only	1.6123	1.0195	13
4th only	1.9975	0.5840	12
2nd & 4th	2.0287	0.2982	8
5th only	1.7000	0.7723	14
2nd & 5th	1.9000	1.0646	9
4th & 5th	1.8986	0.0927	7
all 3 yrs	1.4225	0.3462	8
Overall	2.4444		272

63

$$SS_{group} = \Sigma n_j \left(\bar{X}_j - \bar{X}.. \right)^2$$

$$= 201(2.6774 - 2.4444)^2 + 13(1.6123 - 2.4444)^2 + ... + 8(1.4225 - 2.4444)^2$$

$$= 44.5570$$

MS_{error} = average variance (weighted)

$$= \frac{200 * 0.9450 + 12 * 1.0195 + ... + 7 * 0.3462}{200 + 12 + ... + 7} = 0.8761$$

ANOVA

GPA

	Sum of Squares	df	Mean Square	F	Sig.
Between Groups	44.557	7	6.365	7.266	.000
Within Groups	231.282	264	.876		
Total	275.839	271			

11.19 Square Root Transformation of data in Table 11.6:

Original data:

	Control	0.1	0.5	1	2
	130	93	510	229	144
	94	444	416	475	111
	225	403	154	348	217
	105	192	636	276	200
	92	67	396	167	84
	190	170	451	151	99
	32	77	376	107	44
	64	353	192	235	84
	69	365	384		284
	93	422			293

Means	109.4	258.6	390.56	248.5	156
S.D.	58.5	153.32	147.68	118.74	87.65
Var	3421.82	23506.04	21809.78	14098.86	7682.22
n	10	10	9	8	10

Square root transformed data:

	Control	0.1	0.5	1	2
	11.402	9.644	22.583	15.133	12.000
	9.695	21.071	20.396	21.794	10.536
	15.000	20.075	12.410	18.655	14.731
	10.247	13.856	25.219	16.613	14.142
	9.592	8.185	19.900	12.923	9.165
	13.784	13.038	21.237	12.288	9.950

64

	5.657	8.775	19.391	10.344	6.633
	8.000	18.788	13.856	15.330	9.165
	8.307	19.105	19.596		16.852
	9.644	20.543			17.117
Means	10.13	15.31	19.40	15.39	12.03
S.D.	2.73	5.19	4.00	3.67	3.54
Var	7.48	26.96	16.03	13.49	12.55
n	10	10	9	8	10

11.21 Magnitude of effect for data in Exercise 11.17:

$$\eta^2 = \frac{SS_{group}}{SS_{total}} \qquad\qquad \omega^2 = \frac{SS_{group} - (k-1)MS_{error}}{SS_{total} + MS_{error}}$$

$$= \frac{44.557}{275.839} = .16 \qquad\qquad = \frac{44.557 - (8-1)0.876}{275.839 + 0.876} = .1389$$

11.23 Transforming Time to Speed in Exercise 11.22 involves a reciprocal transformation. The effect of the transformation is to decrease the relative distance between large values.

11.25 The parts of speech (noun vs. verb) are fixed. But the individual items within those parts of speech may well be random, representing a random sample of nouns and a random sample of verbs.

11.27 Analysis of Davey et al. data

Report

dv

group	Mean	N	Std. Deviation
1.00	12.6000	10	6.02218
2.00	7.0000	10	2.98142
3.00	8.7000	10	2.35938
Total	9.4333	30	4.62887

ANOVA

dv

	Sum of Squares	df	Mean Square	F	Sig.
Between Groups	164.867	2	82.433	4.876	.016
Within Groups	456.500	27	16.907		
Total	621.367	29			

11.29 Analysis of Epinuneq.dat, ignoring the effect of Interval. These results come from SPSS.

Descriptives

ERRORS

	N	Mean	Std. Deviation	Std. Error
1	42	3.14	1.52	.24
2	42	4.81	1.25	.19
3	37	2.11	1.51	.25
Total	121	3.40	1.80	.16

ANOVA

ERRORS

	Sum of Squares	df	Mean Square	F	Sig.
Between Groups	147.970	2	73.985	36.197	.000
Within Groups	241.187	118	2.044		
Total	389.157	120			

11.31 Computer exercise. Repeating Exercise 11.29 using Epineq.dat. This output comes from Minitab.

a. Analysis for Interval 1:

```
Analysis of Variance for Errors
Source     DF        SS        MS        F         P
Dosage      2     71.72     35.86     14.93     0.000
Error      33     79.25      2.40
Total      35    150.97
```

```
                                    Individual 95% CIs For Mean
                                    Based on Pooled StDev
                                    ----+---------+---------+---------+--
Level      N      Mean     StDev
1         12     3.167     1.801            (-----*-----)
2         12     5.333     1.073                          (------*-----)
3         12     1.917     1.676    (-----*-----)
                                    ----+---------+---------+---------+--
Pooled StDev =    1.550             1.5       3.0       4.5       6.0
```

b. Analysis for Interval 2:

```
Analysis of Variance for Errors

Source     DF        SS        MS        F         P
Dosage      2     32.06     16.03      8.78     0.001
Error      33     60.25      1.83
Total      35     92.31
```

Individual 95% CIs For Mean

Based on Pooled StDev

```
Level         N      Mean    StDev   ---------+---------+---------+-------
1            12      2.833   1.267            (------*-----)
2            12      4.417   1.379                          (------*-----)
3            12      2.167   1.403   (------*------)
                                     ---------+---------+---------+-------
Pooled StDev =       1.351                   2.4       3.6       4.8
```

c. Analysis for Interval 3:

```
Analysis of Variance for Errors
Source      DF       SS      MS        F       P
Dosage       2      35.06    17.53    7.76    0.002
Error       33      74.58     2.26
Total       35     109.64

                                  Individual 95% CIs For Mean
                                  Based on Pooled StDev
Level        N      Mean    StDev  -+---------+---------+---------+-----
1           12      3.167   1.403             (------*-------)
2           12      4.417   1.311                       (-------*------)
3           12      2.000   1.758  (-------*------)
                                   -+---------+---------+---------+-----
Pooled StDev =      1.503          1.2       2.4       3.6       4.8
```

d. The average of the 9 variances :

$$\bar{s}^2 = \frac{1.801^2 + 1.073^2 + \dots + 1.758^2}{9} = 2.162$$

The average of the three error terms:

$$\text{average}(MS_{error}) = \frac{2.40 + 1.83 + 2.26}{3} = 2.163$$

These two values agree within minor rounding error.

11.33 Gouzoulis-Mayfrank et al. (2000) study:

Descriptives

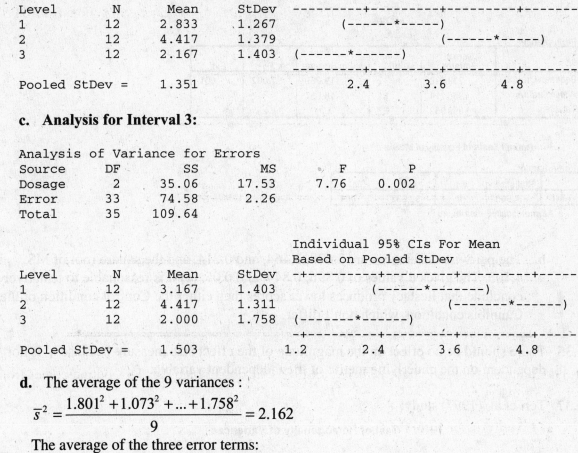

Performance

	N	Mean	Std. Deviation	Std. Error	95% Confidence Interval for Mean		Minimum	Maximum
					Lower Bound	Upper Bound		
Ecstacy	28	25.9286	3.88662	.73450	24.4215	27.4356	18.00	34.00
Control	28	29.6071	4.89398	.92488	27.7095	31.5048	18.00	40.00
Cannibis	28	29.3929	3.39214	.64105	28.0775	30.7082	22.00	37.00
Total	84	28.3095	4.39599	.47964	27.3555	29.2635	18.00	40.00

Test of Homogeneity of Variances

Performance

Levene Statistic	df1	df2	Sig.
1.223	2	81	.300

Performance

	Sum of Squares	df	Mean Square	F	Sig.
Between Groups	238.738	2	119.369	7.082	.001
Within Groups	1365.214	81	16.854		
Total	1603.952	83			

Robust Tests of Equality of Means

Performance

	Statistic[a]	df1	df2	Sig.
Welch	7.565	2	52.932	.001

a. Asymptotically F distributed.

b. The pairwise differences are 3.678, 3.464, and 0.214, and the square root of MS_{error} is 4.105. The gives **d** values of 0.896, 0.844, and 0.05. **(c)** it is reasonable to tentatively conclude that Ecstacy produces lower scores than either the Control condition or the Cannibis condition, which don't differ.

11.35 There should be no effect on the magnitude of the effect size measure because η^2 is not dependent on the underlying metric of the independent variable.

11.37 Teri et al. (1997) study:

Test of Homogeneity of Variances

Change

Levene Statistic	df1	df2	Sig.
1.671	3	68	.181

Descriptives

Change

	N	Mean	Std. Deviation	Std. Error	95% Confidence Interval for Mean	
					Lower Bound	Upper Bound
1.00	23	4.2687	3.81590	.79567	2.6186	5.9188
2.00	19	5.0863	2.94113	.67474	3.6687	6.5039
3.00	10	-.7170	2.92656	.92546	-2.8105	1.3765
4.00	20	.3565	2.65011	.59258	-.8838	1.5968
Total	72	2.7053	3.89648	.45920	1.7897	3.6209

ANOVA

Change

	Sum of Squares	df	Mean Square	F	Sig.
Between Groups	391.391	3	130.464	12.922	.000
Within Groups	686.570	68	10.097		
Total	1077.961	71			

There was considerably, and significantly, more change in the two behavioral treatment groups.

Chapter 12 Multiple Comparisons Among Treatment Means

12.1 The effects of food and water deprivation on a learning task:

a. ANOVA with linear contrasts:

Groups:	ad lib (1)	2/day (2)	food (3)	water (4)	f & w (5)	
Means:	18	24	8	12	11	
a_j:	.5	.5	-.333	-.333	-.333	$0.8333 = \Sigma a_j^2$
b_j:	1	-1	0	0	0	$2 = \Sigma b_j^2$
c_j:	0	0	.5	.5	-1	$1.5 = \Sigma c_j^2$
d_j:	0	0	1	-1	0	$2 = \Sigma d_j^2$

$$\psi_1 = (.5)(18) + (.5)(24) + (-.333)(8) + (-.333)(12)(-.333)(11) = 10.667$$

$$\psi_2 = (1)(18) + (-1)(24) + (0)(8) + (0)(12) + (0)(11) = -6$$

$$\psi_3 = (0)(18) + (0)(24) + (.5)(8) + (.5)(12) + (-1)(11) = -1$$

$$\psi_4 = (0)(18) + (0)(24) + (1)(8) + (-1)(12) + 0(11) = -4$$

$$SS_{contrast_1} = \frac{n\psi_1}{\Sigma a_j^2} = \frac{5(10.667^2)}{0.8333} = 682.667$$

$$SS_{contrast_2} = \frac{n\psi_2}{\Sigma b_j^2} = \frac{5(-6^2)}{2} = 90$$

$$SS_{contrast_3} = \frac{n\psi_3}{\Sigma c_j^2} = \frac{5(-1^2)}{1.5} = 3.333$$

$$SS_{contrast_4} = \frac{n\psi_4}{\Sigma d_j^2} = \frac{5(-4^2)}{2} = 40.000$$

Source	df	SS	MS	F
Deprivation	4	816.000	204.000	36.429*
1&2 vs 3,4,5	1	682.667	682.667	121.905*
1 vs 2	1	90.000	90.000	16.071*
3&4 vs 5	1	3.333	3.333	<1
3 vs 4	1	40.000	40.000	7.143*
Error	20	112.000	5.600	
Total	24	928.000		

$*p < .05 \quad [F_{.05(4,20)} = 2.87; F_{.05(1,20)} = 4.35]$

b. Orthogonality of contrasts:

Cross-products of coefficients:

$$\Sigma a_j b_j = (.5)(1) + (.5)(-1) + (.333)(0) + (.333)(0) + (.333)(0) = 0$$
$$\Sigma a_j c_j = (.5)(0) + (.5)(0) + (.333)(.5) + (.333)(.5) + (.333)(-1) = 0$$
$$\Sigma a_j d_j = (.5)(0) + (.5)(0) + (.333)(1) + (.333)(-1) + (.333)(0) = 0$$
$$\Sigma b_j c_j = (1)(0) + (-1)(0) + (0)(.5) + (0)(.5) + (0)(-1) = 0$$
$$c_j d_j = (0)(0) + (0)(0) + (.5)(1) + (.5)(-1) + (1)(0) = 0$$

c.

$$SS_{treat} = \Sigma SS_{contrast}$$
$$816.000 = 682.667 + 90.000 + 3.333 + 40.000$$

12.3　For $\alpha = .05$:

Per comparison error rate $= \alpha = .05$
Familywise error rate $= 1 - (1 - \alpha)^2 = .0975$.

12.5　Studentized range statistic for data in Exercise 11.2:

$\bar{X}_1 = 19.3 \quad n_1 = 10$

$\bar{X}_2 = 12.0 \quad n_2 = 10$

$$q_2 = \frac{\bar{X}_1 - \bar{X}_2}{\sqrt{\dfrac{MS_{error}}{n}}} = \frac{19.3 - 12.0}{\sqrt{\dfrac{10.56}{10}}} = \frac{7.3}{1.028} = 7.101$$

$q_2 = 7.10 = 5.023 \sqrt{2} = 7.10 = t\sqrt{2}$

12.7 The Bonferroni test on contrasts in Exercise 12.2 (data from Exercise 11.1):

From Exercise 12.2: $\psi_1 = 5.25$ $\psi_2 = 2.40$ $n = 10$

$$\Sigma a_j^2 = 1 \qquad \Sigma b_j^2 = 2 \qquad MS_{error} = 9.67$$

$$t = \frac{\psi}{\sqrt{\dfrac{\Sigma a_j^2 MS_{error}}{n}}}$$

$$t_1' = \frac{5.25}{\sqrt{\dfrac{(1)(9.67)}{10}}} = 5.34 \qquad\qquad t_1' = \frac{2.40}{\sqrt{\dfrac{(2)(9.67)}{10}}} = 1.72$$

$[t_{.05}(df_{error} = 45; 2\,\text{comparisons}) = 2.32)$ Reject H_0 for only the first comparison.

12.9 A post hoc test like the Tukey or the REGWQ often does not get at the specific questions we have in mind, and, at the same time, often answers questions in which we have no interest.

12.11 Scheffé's test on the data in Exercise 12.10:

Group	1	2	3	4	5
$\bar{X}_j$	10	18	19	21	29
n_j	8	5	8	7	9
s_j^2	7.4	8.9	8.6	7.2	9.3
a_j	-16	-16	-16	21	21
b_j	-20	8	8	8	0

$$MS_{error} = \frac{\Sigma(n_j - 1)s_j^2}{\Sigma(n_j - 1)} = 8.2875$$

$$F_{contrast_1} = \frac{L^2}{\Sigma n_j a_j^2 MS_{error}} = \frac{3416^2}{(12432)(8.2875)} = 113.26$$

$$F_{contrast_2} = \frac{L^2}{\Sigma n_j b_j^2 MS_{error}} = \frac{1512^2}{(4480)(8.2875)} = 61.57$$

$$F_{crit} = (k-1)F_{.05(k-1,df_{error})} = 4F_{.05(4,32)} = 4(2.69) = 10.76$$

Thus both contrasts are significant.

12.13 Dunnett's test on data in Table 11.6:

critical value

$$\left(\overline{X}_c - \overline{X}_j\right) = t_d \sqrt{\frac{2MS_{error}}{\overline{n}_h}} = 2.58\sqrt{\frac{2(0.065)}{9.326}} = 0.305$$

The control group is significantly different from the 0.1 µg, the 0.5 µg, and the 1.0 µg groups.

12.15 They are sequentially modified because you change the critical value each time you reject another null hypothesis.

12.17 Conti and Musty (1984) recorded locomotive behavior in rats in response to injection of THC in the an active brain region. The raw data showed a clear linear relationship between group means and standard deviations, but a logarithmic transformation of the data largely removed this relationship. Mean locomotive behavior increased with dosage up to 0.5 µg, but further dose increases resulting in decreased behavior. Polynomial trend analysis revealed no linear trend but a significant quadratic trend.

12.19 If there were significant differences due to Interval and we combined across intervals, those differences would be incorporated into the error term, decreasing power.

12.21 At all three intervals there was a significant linear and quadratic trend, indicating that the effect of epinephrine on memory increases with a moderate dose but then declines with a greater dose. The linear trend reflects the fact that in the high dose condition the animals do even worse than with no epinephrine.

12.23 The first comparison calls for comparing the two control groups with the experimental groups. The solution from SPSS follows for the contrast itself. (SPSS only allows me to specify 1/3 as .33, rather than using more decimal places, which is why it complains that the coefficients don't sum to 0 and gives the contrast as 10.77 rather than 10.6

Contrast Coefficients

Contrast	conditio				
	1.00	2.00	3.00	4.00	5.00
1	.5	.5	-.33	-.33	-.33

Contrast Tests

		Contrast	Value of Contrast	Std. Error	t	df	Sig. (2-tailed)
dv	Assume equal variances	1	10.7700[a]	.96224	11.193	20	.000
	Does not assume equal	1	10.7700[a]	.99539	10.820	14.898	.000

a. The sum of the contrast coefficients is not zero.

The square root of MS_{error} = 2.366, which I will use to compute the confidence interval. I will use 10.67 as the (correct) contrast, even though that is not what SPSS reported. Then

$$CI_{.95} = (\psi) \pm t_{.05} s_{error}$$
$$= (10.67) \pm (2.086)(2.366)$$
$$= (10.67) \pm 4.935$$
$$= 5.735 \le \mu_1 - \mu_2 \le 15.605$$

12.25 The study by Davey et al. (2003):

The group means are Negative mood =12.6, Positive mood = 7.0, No induction = 8.7

The SPSS ONEWAY solution with one contrast comparing the Negative and Positive mood groups is shown below.

ANOVA

Things listed to check

	Sum of Squares	df	Mean Square	F	Sig.
Between Groups	164.867	2	82.433	4.876	.016
Within Groups	456.500	27	16.907		
Total	621.367	29			

Contrast Coefficients

	Group		
Contrast	Negative	Positive	None
1	1	-1	0

Contrast Tests

		Contrast	Value of Contrast	Std. Error	t	df	Sig. (2-tailed)
Things listed to check	Assume equal variances	1	5.6000	1.83888	3.045	27	.005
	Does not assume equal	1	5.6000	2.12498	2.635	13.162	.020

The contrast between the Positive and Negative mood conditions was significant ($t(27)$ = 3.045, $p < .05$). This leads to an effect size of $d = \psi / \sqrt{MS_{error}} = 5.6 / \sqrt{16.907}$
$= 5.6 / 4.11 = 1.36$. The two groups differ by over 1 1/3 standard deviations. It is evident that inducing a negative mood leads to more checking behavior than introducing a positive mood. (If we had compared the Positive and No mood conditions, the difference would not have been significant. However I had not planned to make that comparison.

12.27 This requires students to make up their own example.

74

Chapter 13 - Factorial Analysis of Variance

Note: Because of severe rounding in reporting and using means, there will be visible rounding error in the following answers, when compared to standard computer solutions. I have made the final answer equal the correct answer, even if that meant that it is not exactly the answer to the calculations shown. (e.g. 3(3.3) would be shown as 10.0, not 9.9)

13.1 Mother/infant interaction for primiparous/multiparous mothers under or over 18 years of age with LBW or full-term infants:

Table of cell means

		LBW < 18	LBW > 18	NBW	
Mother's	Primi-	4.5	5.3	6.4	5.40
Parity	Multi-	3.9	6.9	8.2	6.33
		4.2	6.1	7.3	5.87

Size/Age

$$SS_{total} = \sum X^2 - \frac{\left(\sum X\right)^2}{N} = 2404 - \frac{352^2}{60} = 338.93$$

$$SS_{Parity} = ns\Sigma\left(\bar{X}_{i.} - \bar{X}_{..}\right)^2$$

$$= 10(3)[(5.40 - 5.87)^2 + (6.33 - 5.87)^2]$$

$$= 30(0.4356) = 13.067$$

$$SS_{size} = np\Sigma\left(\bar{X}_{.j} - \bar{X}_{..}\right)^2$$

$$= 10(2)[(4.200 - 5.87)^2 + (6.10 - 5.87)^2 + (7.30 - 5.87)^2]$$

$$= 20(2.79 + 0.05 + 2.04) = 20(4.89)$$

$$= 97.733$$

$$SS_{cells} = n\Sigma\left(\bar{X}_{ij} - \bar{X}_{..}\right)^2$$

$$= 10[(4.5 - 5.87)^2 + ... + (8.2 - 5.87)^2]$$

$$= 10(12.853) = 128.53$$

$$SS_{PS} = SS_{cells} - SS_P - SS_S = 128.53 - 13.067 - 97.733$$

$$= 17.733$$

$$SS_{error} = SS_{total} - SS_{cells} = 338.93 - 128.53$$

$$= 210.40$$

Source	df	SS	MS	F
Parity	1	13.067	13.067	3.354
Size/Age	2	97.733	48.867	12.541*
P x S	2	17.733	8.867	2.276
Error	54	210.400	3.896	
Total	59	338.933		

$*p < .05 \quad F_{.05}(2,54) = 3.17$

13.3 The mean for these primiparous mothers would not be expected to be a good estimate of the mean for the population of all primiparous mothers because 50% of the population of primiparous mothers do not give birth to LBW infants. This would be important if we wished to take means from this sample as somehow representing the population means for primiparous and multiparous mothers.

13.5 Memory of avoidance of a fear-producing stimulus:

		Area of Stimulation			
		Neutral	Area A	Area B	Mean
	50	28.6	16.8	24.4	23.27
Delay	100	28.0	23.0	16.0	22.33
	150	28.0	26.8	26.4	27.07
	Mean	28.2	22.2	22.27	24.22

$$\sum X = 1090 \quad \sum X^2 = 28374 \quad N = 45 \quad n_{ij} = 5 \quad a = 3 \quad b = 3$$

$$SS_{total} = \sum X^2 - \frac{\left(\sum X\right)^2}{N} = 28374 - \frac{1090^2}{45} = 1971.778$$

$$SS_{Delay} = na\Sigma\left(\bar{X}_{i.} - \bar{X}_{..}\right)^2$$
$$= 5(3)[(23.27 - 24.22)^2 + (22.33 - 24.22)^2 + (27.07 - 24.22)^2]$$
$$= 5(3)(0.90 + 3.57 + 8.12) = 30(12.60)$$
$$= 188.578$$

$$SS_{Area} = nd\Sigma\left(\bar{X}_{.j} - \bar{X}_{..}\right)^2$$
$$= 5(3)[(28.20 - 24.22)^2 + (22.20 - 24.22)^2 + (22.27 - 24.22)^2]$$
$$= 356.044$$

$$SS_{Cells} = n\Sigma\left(\bar{X}_{ij} - \bar{X}_{..}\right)^2$$
$$= 5[(28.60 - 24.22)^2 + (16.80 - 24.22)^2 + ... + (26.4 - 24.22)^2]$$
$$= 916.578$$

76

$$SS_{DA} = SS_{cells} - SS_D - SS_A = 916.578 - 188.578 - 356.044 = 371.956$$

$$SS_{error} = SS_{total} - SS_{cells} = 1971.778 - 916.578 = 1055.200$$

Source	df	SS	MS	F
Delay	2	188.578	94.289	3.22
Area	2	356.044	178.022	6.07*
D x A	4	371.956	92.989	3.17*
Error	36	1055.200	29.311	
Total	44	1971.778		

$*p < .05 \quad [F_{.05(2,36)} = 3.27; F_{.05(4,36)} = 2.64]$

13.7 In Exercise 13.5, if A refers to Area:

$\hat{\alpha}_1$ = the treatment effect for the Neutral site

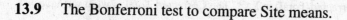

$$= \bar{X}_{.1} - \bar{X}_{..}$$

$$= 28.2 - 24.22 = 3.978$$

13.9 The Bonferroni test to compare Site means.

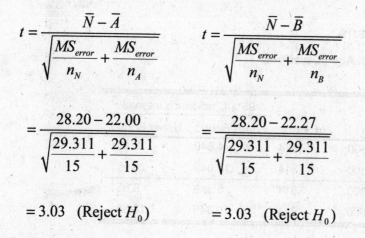

$$t = \frac{\bar{N} - \bar{A}}{\sqrt{\dfrac{MS_{error}}{n_N} + \dfrac{MS_{error}}{n_A}}} \qquad t = \frac{\bar{N} - \bar{B}}{\sqrt{\dfrac{MS_{error}}{n_N} + \dfrac{MS_{error}}{n_B}}}$$

$$= \frac{28.20 - 22.00}{\sqrt{\dfrac{29.311}{15} + \dfrac{29.311}{15}}} \qquad = \frac{28.20 - 22.27}{\sqrt{\dfrac{29.311}{15} + \dfrac{29.311}{15}}}$$

$$= 3.03 \quad (\text{Reject } H_0) \qquad\qquad = 3.03 \quad (\text{Reject } H_0)$$

$[t'_{.025}(2,36) = \pm 2.34]$

We can conclude that both the difference between Groups N and A and between Groups N and B are significant, and our familywise error rate will not exceed $\alpha = .05$.

13.11 Rerunning Exercise 11.3 as a factorial design:

The following printout is from SPSS

Tests of Between-Subjects Effects

Dependent Variable: Recall

Source	Type III Sum of Squares	df	Mean Square	F	Sig.
Corrected Model	1059.800[a]	3	353.267	53.301	.000
Intercept	5017.600	1	5017.600	757.056	.000
Age	115.600	1	115.600	17.442	.000
LevelProc	792.100	1	792.100	119.512	.000
Age * LevelProc	152.100	1	152.100	22.949	.000
Error	238.600	36	6.628		
Total	6316.000	40			
Corrected Total	1298.400	39			

a. R Squared = .816 (Adjusted R Squared = .801)

[The Corrected Model is the sum of the main effects and interaction. The Intercept is the correction factor, which is $(\Sigma X)^2$. The Total (as opposed to Corrected Total) is ΣX^2. The Corrected Total is what we have called Total.]

Estimated Marginal Means

3. Age * LevelProc

Dependent Variable: Recall

Age	LevelProc	Mean	Std. Error	95% Confidence Interval	
				Lower Bound	Upper Bound
1.00	1.00	6.500	.814	4.849	8.151
	2.00	19.300	.814	17.649	20.951
2.00	1.00	7.000	.814	5.349	8.651
	2.00	12.000	.814	10.349	13.651

The results show that there is a significance difference between younger and older subjects, that there is better recall in tasks which require more processing, and that there is an interaction between age and level of processing (LevelProc). The difference between the two levels of processing is greater for the younger subjects than it is for the older ones, primarily because the older ones do not do much better with greater amounts of processing.

13.13 Made-up data with main effects but no interaction:

Cell means: 8   12
                  4   6

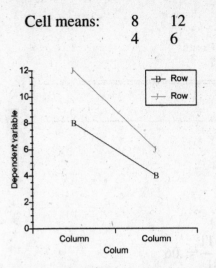

13.15 The interaction was of primary interest in an experiment by Nisbett in which he showed that obese people varied the amount of food they consumed depending on whether a lot or a little food was visible, while normal weight subjects ate approximately the same amount under the two conditions.

13.17 Magnitude of effect for mother-infant interaction data in Exercise 13.1:

$$\eta_P^2 = \frac{SS_{parity}}{SS_{total}} = \frac{13.067}{338.933} = .04$$

$$\eta_s^2 = \frac{SS_{size}}{SS_{total}} = \frac{97.733}{338.933} = .29$$

$$\eta_{Ps}^2 = \frac{SS_{ps}}{SS_{total}} = \frac{17.733}{338.933} = .05$$

$$\omega_p^2 = \frac{SS_{parity} - (p-1)MS_{error}}{SS_{total} + MS_{errpr}} = \frac{13.067 - (1)3.896}{338.933 + 3.896} = .03$$

$$\omega_s^2 = \frac{SS_{size} - (s-1)MS_{error}}{SS_{total} + MS_{errpr}} = \frac{97.733 - (2)3.896}{338.933 + 3.896} = .26$$

$$\omega_{ps}^2 = \frac{SS_{ps} - (p-1)(s-1)MS_{error}}{SS_{total} + MS_{errpr}} = \frac{17.733 - (1)(2)3.896}{338.933 + 3.896} = .03$$

13.19 Magnitude of effect for avoidance learning data in Exercise 13.5:

$$\eta_D^2 = \frac{SS_{delay}}{SS_{total}} = \frac{188.578}{1971.778} = .10$$

$$\eta_A^2 = \frac{SS_{area}}{SS_{total}} = \frac{356.044}{1971.778} = .18$$

$$\eta_{DA}^2 = \frac{SS_{DA}}{SS_{total}} = \frac{17.733}{1971.778} = .19$$

$$\omega_D^2 = \frac{SS_{delay} - (d-1)MS_{error}}{SS_{total} + MS_{errpr}} = \frac{188.578 - (2)29.311}{1971.778 + 29.311} = .06$$

$$\omega_A^2 = \frac{SS_{area} - (a-1)MS_{error}}{SS_{total} + MS_{errpr}} = \frac{356.044 - (2)29.311}{1971.778 + 29.311} = .15$$

$$\omega_{DA}^2 = \frac{SS_{DA} - (d-1)(a-1)MS_{error}}{SS_{total} + MS_{errpr}} = \frac{371.956 - (2)(2)29.311}{1971.778 + 29.311} = .13$$

13.21 Three-way ANOVA on Early Experience x Intensity of UCS x Conditioned Stimulus (Tone or Vibration):

$n = 5$ in all cells $\qquad$ SS$_{total}$ = 41,151.00

E×I×C Cells

Exper:	Hi	Med	Low		CS = Tone		Hi	Med	Low			
Control	11	16	21	12.0			19	24	29	24.00	20.00
Tone	25	28	34	29.0			21	26	31	26.00	27.50
Vib	6	13	20	13.0			40	41	52	44.33	28.67
Both	22	30	30	27.33			35	38	48	40.33	33.83
	16	21.75	105	21.33			28.75	32.25	40.00	33.66	27.50

CS = Tone $\qquad\qquad\qquad\qquad\qquad\qquad$ CS = Vibration

E×I Cells $\qquad\qquad\qquad$ Intensity

Experience:	High	Med	Low	
Control	15	20	25	20.00
Tone	23	27	32.5	27.50
Vib	23	27	36	28.67
Both	28.5	34	39	33.83
	22.38	27.00	33.12	27.50

E×C Cells

Experience:	Conditioned Stimulus		
	Tone	Vib	
Control	16.00	24.00	20.00
Tone	29.00	26.00	27.50
Vib	13.00	44.33	28.67
Both	27.33	40.33	33.83
	21.33	33.66	27.50

I×C Cells

Intensity:	Conditioned Stim		
	Tone	Vib	
High	16.00	28.75	22.38
Med	21.75	32.25	27.00
Low	26.25	40.00	33.12
	21.33	33.67	27.50

$$SS_E = nic\Sigma\left(\bar{X}_{i..} - \bar{X}_{...}\right)^2 = 5(3)(2)\left[\begin{array}{c}(20-27.5)^2 + (27.5-27.5)^2 + \\ (28.67-27.5)^2 + (33.83-27.5)^2\end{array}\right]$$

$$= 2931.667$$

$$SS_I = nec\Sigma\left(\bar{X}_{.j.} - \bar{X}_{...}\right)^2 = 5(4)(2)\left[(22.38-27.5)^2 + (27.00-27.5)^2 + (33.12-27.5)^2\right]$$

$$= 2326.250$$

$$SS_{cellsEI} = nc\Sigma\left(\bar{X}_{ij.} - \bar{X}_{...}\right)^2 = (5)(2)\left[(15.00-27.50)^2 + ... + (39.00-27.50)^2\right]$$

$$= 5325.000$$

$$SS_{E\times I} = SS_{cellsEI} - SS_E - SS_I = 5325.000 - 2931.667 - 2326.250 = 67.083$$

$$SS_C = nei\Sigma\left(\bar{X}_{..k} - \bar{X}_{...}\right)^2 = 5(4)(3)\left[(21.33-27.5)^2 + (33.66-27.5)^2\right]$$

$$= 4563.333$$

$$SS_{cellsEC} = ni\Sigma\left(\bar{X}_{i.k} - \bar{X}_{...}\right)^2 = (5)(3)\left[(16.00-27.50)^2 + ... + (40.33-27.50)^2\right]$$

$$= 12,110.000$$

$$SS_{E\times C} = SS_{cellsEC} - SS_E - SS_C = 12,110.000 - 2931.667 - 4563.333 = 4615.000$$

$$SS_{cellsIC} = ne\Sigma\left(\bar{X}_{ij.} - \bar{X}_{...}\right)^2 = (5)(4)\left[(15.00 - 27.50)^2 + ... + (39.00 - 27.50)^2\right]$$
$$= 6945.000$$

$$SS_{I \times C} = SS_{cellsIC} - SS_I - SS_C = 6945.000 - 2326.250 - 4563.333 = 55.417$$

$$SS_{cellsEIC} = n\Sigma\left(\bar{X}_{ijk} - \bar{X}_{...}\right)^2 = (5)\left[(11.00 - 27.50)^2 + ... + (48.00 - 27.50)^2\right]$$
$$= 14,680.000$$

$$SS_{E \times I \times C} = SS_{cellsEIC} - SS_E - SS_I - SS_C - SS_{EI} - SS_{EC} - SS_{IC}$$
$$= 14,680.000 - 2931.667 - 2326.250 - 4563.333 - 67.083 - 4615.000 - 55.417$$
$$= 121.25$$

$$SS_{error} = SS_{total} - SS_{CellsC \times E \times I} = 41,151.000 - 14,680.000 = 26.471.000$$

Source	df	SS	MS	F
Experience	3	2931.667	977.222	3.544*
Intensity	2	2326.250	1163.125	4.218*
Cond Stim	1	4563.333	4563.333	16.550*
E x I	6	67.083	11.181	<1
E x C	3	4615.000	1538.333	5.579*
I x C	2	55.417	27.708	<1
E x I x C	6	121.250	20.208	<1
Error	96	26,471.000	275.740	
Total	119	41,151.000		

*$p < .05$ [$F_{.05(1,96)} = 3.94$; $F_{.05(2,96)} = 3.09$; $F_{.05(3,96)} = 2.70$; $F_{.05(6,96)} = 2.19$]

There are significant main effects for all variables with a significant Experience × Conditioned Stimulus interaction.

13.23 Analysis of Epineq.dat:

Tests of Between-Subjects Effects

Dependent Variable: Trials to reversal

Source	Type III Sum of Squares	df	Mean Square	F	Sig.
Corrected Model	141.130[a]	8	17.641	8.158	.000
Intercept	1153.787	1	1153.787	533.554	.000
DOSE	133.130	2	66.565	30.782	.000
DELAY	2.296	2	1.148	.531	.590
DOSE * DELAY	5.704	4	1.426	.659	.622
Error	214.083	99	2.162		
Total	1509.000	108			
Corrected Total	355.213	107			

a. R Squared = .397 (Adjusted R Squared = .349)

13.25 Tukey on Dosage data from Exercise 13.25

Multiple Comparisons

Dependent Variable: Trials to reversal
Tukey HSD

(I) dosage of epinephrine	(J) dosage of epinephrine	Mean Difference (I-J)	Std. Error	Sig.
0.0 mg/kg	0.3 mg/kg	-1.67*	.35	.000
	1.0 mg/kg	1.03*	.35	.010
0.3 mg/kg	0.0 mg/kg	1.67*	.35	.000
	1.0 mg/kg	2.69*	.35	.000
1.0 mg/kg	0.0 mg/kg	-1.03*	.35	.010
	0.3 mg/kg	-2.69*	.35	.000

Based on observed means.

*. The mean difference is significant at the .05 level.

All of these groups differed from each other at $p \leq .05$.

13.27 Simple effects on data in Exercise 13.26.

Source	df	SS	MS	F
Condition	1	918.750	918.75	34.42*
Cond @ Inexp.	1	1014.00	1014.00	37.99*
Cond @ Exp.	1	121.50	121.50	4.55*
Cond*Exper	1	216.750	216.75	8.12*
Other Effects	9	2631.417		
Error	36	961.000	26.694	
Total	47	4727.917		

*P < .05 [$F_{.05(1.36)}$ = 4.12]

83

13.29 Dress codes and Performance:

$$SS_{total} = \Sigma\left(X - \bar{X}_{..}\right)^2$$
$$= (91 - 72.050)^2 + (78 - 72.050)^2 + ... + (56 - 72.050)^2$$
$$= 13554.65$$

$$SS_{Code} = nc\Sigma\left(\bar{X}_{i.} - \bar{X}..\right)^2$$
$$= 10 * 7[(73.929 - 72.050)^2 + (70.171 - 72.050)^2]$$
$$= 494.290$$

$$SS_{School(Yes)} = n\Sigma\left(\bar{X}_{.j} - \bar{X}..\right)^2$$
$$= 10[(79.7 - 73.929)^2 + (71.5 - 73.929)^2 + ... + (73.5 - 73.929)^2]$$
$$= 10(147.414) = 1474.14$$

$$SS_{School(No)} = n\Sigma\left(\bar{X}_{.j} - \bar{X}..\right)^2$$
$$= 10[(68.5 - 70.171)^2 + (73.7 - 70.171)^2 + ... + (71.1 - 70.171)^2]$$
$$= 10(126.314) = 1263.14$$

$$SS_{School(Code)} = SS_{School(Yes)} + SS_{School(No)} = 1474.14 + 1263.14 = 2737.28$$

$$SS_{error} = SS_{total} - SS_C - SS_{S(C)} = 13554.65 - 494.29 - 2737.28 = 10323.08$$

Source	df	SS	MS	F
Code	1	494.290	494.290	2.166
Error$_1$	12	2737.280	228.107	
School(Code)	12	2737.280	288.107	2.784*
Error$_2$	126	10323.08	81.931	
Total	139	13554.65		

* $p < .05$

The F for Code is not significant but the F for the nested effect is. But notice that the two F values are not all that far apart but their p values are very different. The reason for this is that we only have 12 df for error to test Code, but 126 df for error to test School(Code).

13.31 Gartlett & Bos (2010) Same versus opposite sex parents. Cell means with variances in parentheses.

	Males	Females	
Same-Sex	25.80 (12.96)	26.30 (25.00)	26.05
Opposite-Sex	23.00 (16.00)	20.30 (20.25)	21.65
	24.40	23.3	

$$SS_{Parents} = 2(43)[(26.05 - 23.85)^2 + (21.65 - 23.85)^2] = 832.48$$

$$SS_{Gender} = 2(43)[(24.40 - 23.85)^2 + (23.3 - 23.85)^2] = 52.03$$

$$SS_{Cells} = (43)[(25.8 - 23.85)^2 + (26.3 - 23.85)^2 + (23.00 - 23.85)^2 + 20.3 - 23.85^2]$$
$$= 994.59$$

$$SS_{P*G} = 944.59 - 832.48 - 52.03 = 110.08$$

$$MS_{error} = (12.96 + 25.00 + 16.00 + 20.25)/4 = 18.55$$

Source	df	SS	MS	F
Parents	1	832.38	832.38	44.87*
Gender	1	52.03	52.03	2.80
P*G	1	110.08	110.08	5.93*
Error₂	168		18.55	
Total	171			

* $p < .05$

There is a significant effect due to Same-Sex versus Opposite-Sex parents, with those children raised by Same-Sex couples showing higher levels of competence. There is no effect due to the gender of the child, but there is an interaction, with the male versus female difference being greater in the Opposite-sex condition.

13.33 This question does not have a specific answer.

Chapter 14 – Repeated-Measures Designs

[As in previous chapters, there will be substantial rounding in these answers. I have attempted to make the answers fit with the correct values, rather than the exact results of the specific calculations shown here. Thus I may round cell means to two decimals, but calculation is carried out with many more decimals.]

14.1 Does taking the GRE repeatedly lead to higher scores?

    a. Statistical model:

$$X_{ij} = \mu + \pi_i + \tau_j + \pi\tau_{ij} + e_{ij} \quad \text{or} \quad X_{ij} = \mu + \pi_i + \tau_j + e_{ij}$$

    b. Analysis:

Subject	Mean		Test Session	Mean
1	566.67		1	552.50
2	450.00		2	563.75
3	616.67		3	573.75
4	663.33			
5	436.67			
6	696.67			
7	503.33			
8	573.33			
Mean	563.33			

$$SS_{total} = \sum X^2 - \frac{\left(\sum X\right)^2}{N} = 7811200 - \frac{(13520)^2}{24} = 194933.33$$

$$SS_{subj} = t\Sigma\left(\bar{X}_{i.} - \bar{X}_{..}\right)^2$$

$$= 3[(566.67 - 563.33)^2 + ... + (573.33 - 563.33)^2] = 3(63222.22) = 189,666.67$$

$$SS_{test} = n\Sigma\left(\bar{X}_{.j} - \bar{X}_{..}\right)^2 = 8[(552.50 - 563.33)^2 + (563.75 - 563.33)^2 + (573.75 - 563.33)^2]$$

$$= 8[226.04] = 1808.33$$

$$SS_{error} = SS_{total} - SS_{subj} - SS_{test}$$

$$= 194,933.33 - 189,666.67 - 1808.33 = 3458.33$$

Source	df	SS	MS	F
Subjects	7	189,666.66		
Within subj	16	5266.67		
Test session	2	1808.33	904.17	3.66 ns
Error	14	3458.33	247.02	
Total	23	194,933.33		

14.3 Teaching of self-care skills to severely retarded children:

Cell means:

		Phase		Mean
		Baseline	Training	
Group:	Exp	4.80	7.00	5.90
	Control	4.70	6.40	5.55
	Mean	4.75	6.70	5.72

Subject means:

Grp		S_1	S_2	S_3	S_4	S_5	S_6	S_7	S_8	S_9	S_{10}
	Exp	8.5	6.0	2.5	6.0	5.5	6.5	6.5	5.5	5.5	6.5
	Control	4.0	5.0	9.0	3.5	4.0	8.0	7.5	4.5	5.0	5.5

$$\Sigma X^2 = 1501 \quad \Sigma X = 229 \quad N = 40 \quad n = 10 \quad g = 2 \quad p = 2$$

$$SS_{total} = \sum X^2 - \frac{(\sum X)^2}{N} = 1501 - \frac{229^2}{40} = 189.975$$

$$SS_{subj} = p\Sigma\left(\bar{X}_{ij.} - \bar{X}_{...}\right)^2$$
$$= 2[(8.5-5.72)^2 + ... + (5.5-5.72)^2] = 106.475$$

$$SS_{group} = pn\Sigma\left(\bar{X}_{..k} - \bar{X}_{...}\right)^2$$
$$= 2(8)[(5.90-5.72)^2 + (5.55-5.72)^2] = 1.225$$

$$SS_{phase} = gn\Sigma\left(\bar{X}_{.j.} - \bar{X}_{...}\right)^2$$
$$= 2(10)[(4.75-5.72)^2 + (6.70-5.72)^2] = 38.025$$

$$SS_{cells} = n\Sigma\left(\bar{X}_{.jk} - \bar{X}_{...}\right)^2$$
$$= 10\left[(4.80-5.72)^2 + ... + (6.40-5.72)^2\right] = 39.875$$

$$SS_{PG} = SS_{cells} - SS_{phase} - SS_{group} = 39.875 - 38.025 - 1.225 = 0.925$$

Source	df	SS	MS	F
Between Subj	19	106.475		
Groups	1	1.125	1.125	0.19
Ss w/in Grps	18	105.250	5.847	
Within Subj	20	83.500		
Phase	1	38.025	38.025	15.26*
P x G	1	0.625	0.625	0.25
P x Ss w/in Grps	18	44.850	2.492	
Total	39	189.975		

$*p < .05 \quad [F_{.05(1,18)} = 4.41]$

There is a significant difference between baseline and training, but there are no group differences nor a group x phase interaction.

14.5 Adding a No Attention control group to the study in Exercise 14.3:

Cell means:

		Phase		
		Baseline	Training	Total
Group	Exp	4.8	7.0	5.90
	Att Cont	4.7	6.4	5.55
	No Att Cont	5.1	4.6	4.85
	Total	4.87	6.00	5.43

Subject means:

Group:		S_1	S_2	S_3	S_4	S_5	S_6	S_7	S_8	S_9	S_{10}
	Exp	8.5	6.0	2.5	6.0	5.5	6.5	6.5	5.5	5.5	6.5
	Att Cont	4.0	5.0	9.0	3.5	4.0	8.0	7.5	4.5	5.0	5.0
	No Att Cont	3.5	5.0	7.0	5.5	4.5	6.5	6.5	4.5	2.5	3.0

$$\sum X^2 = 2026 \quad \Sigma X = 326 \quad N = 60 \quad n = 10 \quad g = 3 \quad p = 2$$

$$SS_{total} = \sum X^2 - \frac{\left(\sum X\right)^2}{N} = 2026 - \frac{326^2}{60} = 254.7333$$

$$SS_{subj} = p\Sigma\left(\bar{X}_{ij.} - \bar{X}_{...}\right)^2$$
$$= 2[(8.5 - 5.43)^2 + ... + (3.0 - 5.43)^2] = 159.733$$

$$SS_{group} = pn\Sigma\left(\bar{X}_{..k} - \bar{X}_{...}\right)^2$$
$$= 2(8)[(5.90 - 5.43)^2 + (5.55 - 5.43)^2 + (4.85 - 5.43)^2] = 11.433$$

$$SS_{phase} = gn\Sigma\left(\bar{X}_{.j.} - \bar{X}_{...}\right)^2$$
$$= 3(10)[(4.87 - 5.43)^2 + (6.00 - 5.43)^2] = 19.267$$

$$SS_{cells} = n\Sigma\left(\bar{X}_{.jk} - \bar{X}_{...}\right)^2$$
$$= 10\left[(4.80 - 5.43)^2 + ... + (4.60 - 5.43)^2\right] = 52.333$$

$$SS_{PG} = SS_{cells} - SS_{phase} - SS_{group} = 51.333 - 19.267 - 11.433 = 20.633$$

Source	df	SS	MS	F
Between subj	29	159.7333		
Groups	2	11.4333	5.7166	1.04
Ss w/ Grps	27	148.300	5.4926	
Within subj	30	95.0000		
Phase	1	19.2667	19.2667	9.44*
P * G	2	20.6333	10.3165	5.06*
P * Ss w/Grps	27	55.1000	2.0407	
Total	59	254.733		

*$p < .05$ $[F_{.05(1,27)} = 4.22; F_{.05(2,27)} = 3.36]$

88

b. Plot:

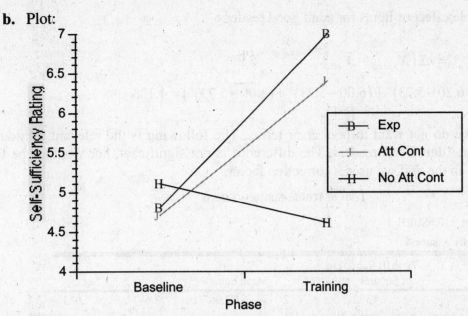

c. There seems to be no difference between the Experimental and Attention groups, but both show significantly more improvement than the No Attention group.

14.7 From Exercise 14.6:

a. Simple effect of reading ability for children:

$$SS_{RatC} = in\Sigma \left(\bar{X}_{RatC} - \bar{X}_C \right)^2$$

$$= 3(5)[(4.80-3.50)^2 + (2.20-3.50)^2] = 50.70$$

$$MS_{RatC} = \frac{SS_{RatC}}{df_{RatC}} = \frac{50.70}{1} = 50.70$$

Because we are using only the data from Children, it would be wise not to use a pooled error term. The following is the relevant printout from SPSS for the Between-subject effect of Reader.

Tests of Between-Subjects Effects[a]

Measure: MEASURE_1

Transformed Variable: Average

Source	Type III Sum of Squares	df	Mean Square	F	Sig.
Intercept	367.500	1	367.500	84.483	.000
READERS	50.700	1	50.700	11.655	.009
Error	34.800	8	4.350		

a. AGE = Children

b. Simple effect of items for adult good readers:

$$SS_{I\,at\,AG} = n\Sigma\left(\bar{X}_{I\,at\,AG} - \bar{X}_{AG}\right)^2$$
$$= 5[(6.20-5.73)^2 + (6.00-5.73)^2 + (5.00-5.73)^2] = 4.133$$

Again, we do not want to pool error terms. The following is the relevant printout from SPSS for Adult Good readers. The difference is not significant, nor would it be for any decrease in the *df* if we used a correction factor.

Tests of Within-Subjects Effects

Measure: MEASURE_1

Sphericity Assumed

Source	Type III Sum of Squares	df	Mean Square	F	Sig.
ITEMS	4.133	2	2.067	3.647	.075
Error(ITEMS)	4.533	8	.567		

14.9 It would certainly affect the covariances because we would force a high level of covariance among items. As the number of responses classified at one level of Item went up, another item would have to go down.

14.11 Plot of results in Exercise 14.10:

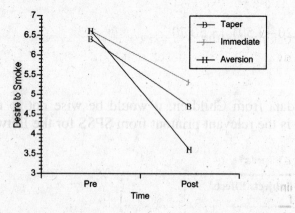

14.13 Analysis of data in Exercise 14.5 by BMDP:

a. Comparison with results obtained by hand in Exercise 14.5.

b. The *F* for Mean is a test on H_0: $\mu = 0$.

c. $MS_{w/in\,Cell}$ is the average of the cell variances.

14.15 Source column of summary table for 4-way ANOVA with repeated measures on A & B and independent measures on C & D.

Source
Between Ss
   C
   D
   CD
   Ss w/in groups
Within Ss
   A
   AC
   AD
   ACD
   A x Ss w/in groups
   B
   BC
   BD
   BCD
   B x Ss w/in groups
   AB
   ABC
   ABD
   ABCD
   AB x Ss w/in groups
Total

14.17 Using the mixed models procedure on data from Exercise 14.16

If we assume that sphericity is a reasonable assumption, we could run the analysis with covtype(cs). That will give us the following, and we can see that the F's are the same as they were in our analysis above.

Fixed Effects

Type III Tests of Fixed Effects[a]

Source	Numerator df	Denominator df	F	Sig.
Intercept	1	42.000	450.019	.000
Group	2	42.000	3.749	.032
Time	2	84	73.534	.000
Group * Time	4	84	4.058	.005

a. Dependent Variable: dv.

However, the correlation matrix below would make us concerned about the reasonableness of a sphericity assumption. (This matrix is collapsed over groups, but reflects the separate matrices well.) Therefore we will assume an autoregressive model for our correlations.

Correlations

		Pre	Post	Followup
Pre	Pearson Correlation	1.000	.585[**]	.282
Post	Pearson Correlation	.585[**]	1.000	.616[**]
Followup	Pearson Correlation	.282	.616[**]	1.000

[**]. Correlation is significant at the 0.01 level (2-tailed).

Fixed Effects

Type III Tests of Fixed Effects[a]

Source	Numerator df	Denominator df	F	Sig.
Intercept	1	43.256	422.680	.000
Group	2	43.256	3.521	.038
Time	2	81.710	71.356	.000
Group * Time	4	81.710	5.578	.001

a. Dependent Variable: dv.

These F values are reasonably close, but certainly not the same.

14.19 Mixed model analysis with unequal size example.

Fixed Effects

Type III Tests of Fixed Effects[a]

Source	Numerator df	Denominator df	F	Sig.
Intercept	1	41.724	393.118	.000
Group	2	41.724	2.877	.068
Time	2	70.480	64.760	.000
Group * Time	4	70.459	5.266	.001

a. Dependent Variable: dv.

Notice that we have a substantial change in the F for Time, though it is still large.

14.21 Everitt's study of anorexia:

a. SPSS printout on gain scores:

Tests of Between-Subjects Effects

Dependent Variable: GAIN

Source	Type III Sum of Squares	df	Mean Square	F	Sig.
Corrected Model	614.644[a]	2	307.322	5.422	.006
Intercept	732.075	1	732.075	12.917	.001
TREAT	614.644	2	307.322	5.422	.006
Error	3910.742	69	56.677		
Total	5075.400	72			
Corrected Total	4525.386	71			

a. R Squared = .136 (Adjusted R Squared = .111)

b. SPSS printout using pretest and posttest:

Tests of Within-Subjects Effects

Measure: MEASURE_1

Sphericity Assumed

Source	Type III Sum of Squares	df	Mean Square	F	Sig.
TIME	366.037	1	366.037	12.917	.001
TIME * TREAT	307.322	2	153.661	5.422	.006
Error(TIME)	1955.371	69	28.339		

c. The *F* comparing groups on gain scores is exactly the same as the *F* for the interaction in the repeated measures design.

d.

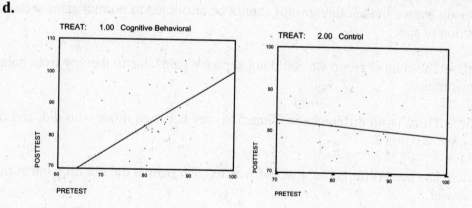

93

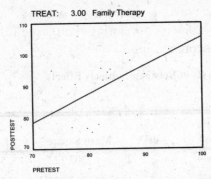

TREAT: 3.00 Family Therapy

The plots show that there is quite a different relationship between the variables in the different groups.

e. Treatment Group = Control

One-Sample Statistics[a]

	N	Mean	Std. Deviation	Std. Error Mean
GAIN	26	-.4500	7.9887	1.5667

a. Treatment Group = Control

One-Sample Test[a]

					95% Confidence Interval of the Difference	
				Mean		
	t	df	Sig. (2-tailed)	Difference	Lower	Upper
GAIN	-.287	25	.776	-.4500	-3.6767	2.7767

a. Treatment Group = Control

This group did not gain significantly over the course of the study. This suggests that any gain we see in the other groups cannot be attributed to normal gains seen as a function of age.

f. Without the control group we could not separate gains due to therapy from gains due to maturation.

14.23 t = -0.555. There is no difference in Time 1 scores between those who did, and did not, have a score at Time 2.

b. If there had been differences, I would worried that people did not drop out at random. to answer.

14.25 Differences due to Judges play an important role.

94

14.27 If I were particularly interested in differences between subjects, and recognized that judges probably didn't have a good anchoring point, and if this lack was not meaningful, I would not be interested in considering it.

14.29 Strayer et al. (2006)

Tests of Between-Subjects Effects

Measure:MEASURE_1
Transformed Variable:Average

Source	Type III Sum of Squares	df	Mean Square	F	Sig.
Intercept	7.711E7	1	7.711E7	724.691	.000
Error	4149966.533	39	106409.398		

Tests of Within-Subjects Effects

Measure:MEASURE_1

Source		Type III Sum of Squares	df	Mean Square	F	Sig.
Condition	Sphericity Assumed	134696.067	2	67348.033	4.131	.020
	Greenhouse-Geisser	134696.067	1.992	67619.134	4.131	.020
	Huynh-Feldt	134696.067	2.000	67348.033	4.131	.020
	Lower-bound	134696.067	1.000	134696.067	4.131	.049
Error(Condition)	Sphericity Assumed	1271689.267	78	16303.709		
	Greenhouse-Geisser	1271689.267	77.687	16369.337		
	Huynh-Feldt	1271689.267	78.000	16303.709		
	Lower-bound	1271689.267	39.000	32607.417		

b. Contrasts on means:

Because the variances within each condition are so similar, I have used $MS_{error(within)}$ as my error term. The means are 776.95, 778.95, and 849.00 for Baseline, Alcohol, and Cell phone conditions, respectively..

$$t = \frac{\hat{\psi}}{\sqrt{\dfrac{\Sigma a_i^2 MS_{error}}{n}}}$$

$$\hat{\psi}_{1vs2} = 776.95 - 778.95 = 2$$

$$\hat{\psi}_{1vs3} = 776.95 - 849.00 = 72.05$$

$$\hat{\psi}_{2vs3} = 778.95 - 849.00 = 70.5$$

$$den = \sqrt{\frac{\Sigma a_i^2 MS_{error}}{n}} = \sqrt{\frac{2 \times 16303.709}{40}} = 28.551$$

$$t_{1vs2} = 2 / 28.551 = 0.07$$

$$t_{1vs3} = 72.05 / 28.551 = 2.52^*$$

$$t_{2vs3} = 70.05 / 28.551 = 2.45^*$$

95

Both Baseline and Alcohol conditions show poorer performance than the cell phone condition, but, interestingly, the Baseline and Alcohol conditions do not differ from each other.

Chapter 15 - Multiple Regression

15.1   Predicting Quality of Life:

    a. All other variables held constant, a difference of +1 degree in Temperature is associated with a difference of −.01 in perceived Quality of Life. A difference of $1000 in median Income, again all other variables held constant, is associated with a +.05 difference in perceived Quality of Life. A similar interpretation applies to b_3 and b_4. Since values of 0.00 cannot reasonably occur for all predictors, the intercept has no meaningful interpretation.

    b.
$$\hat{Y} = 5.37 - .01(55) + .05(12) + .003(500) - .01(200) = 4.92$$

    c.
$$\hat{Y} = 5.37 - .01(55) + .05(12) + .003(100) - .01(200) = 3.72$$

15.3   The F values for the four regression coefficients would be as follows:

$$F_1 = \left[\frac{\beta_1}{s_{\beta_1}}\right]^2 = \left[\frac{-0.438}{0.397}\right]^2 = 1.22 \qquad F_2 = \left[\frac{\beta_2}{s_{\beta_2}}\right]^2 = \left[\frac{0.762}{0.252}\right]^2 = 9.14$$

$$F_3 = \left[\frac{\beta_3}{s_{\beta_3}}\right]^2 = \left[\frac{0.081}{0.052}\right]^2 = 2.43 \qquad F_4 = \left[\frac{\beta_4}{s_{\beta_4}}\right]^2 = \left[\frac{-0.132}{0.025}\right]^2 = 27.88$$

    I would thus delete Temperature, since it has the smallest F, and therefore the smallest semi-partial correlation with the dependent variable.

15.5   **a.** Envir has the largest semi-partial correlation with the criterion, because it has the largest value of t.

    b. The gain in prediction (from $r = .58$ to $R = .697$) which we obtain by using all the predictors is more than offset by the loss of power we sustain as p became large relative to N.

15.7   As the correlation between two variables decreases, the amount of variance in a third variable that they share decreases. Thus the higher will be the possible squared semi-partial correlation of each variable with the criterion. They each can account for more previously unexplained variation.

15.9   The tolerance column shows us that NumSup and Respon are fairly well correlated with the other predictors, whereas Yrs is nearly independent of them.

15.11 Using Y and $\hat{Y}$ from Exercise 15.10:

$$MS_{residual} = \frac{\sum \left(Y - \hat{Y}\right)^2}{N-p-1}$$

$$= \frac{42.322}{15-4-1} = 4.232 \quad \text{(also calculated by BMDP in Exercise 15.4)}$$

15.13 Adjusted R^2 for 15 cases in Exercise 15.12:

$$R^2_{0.1234} = .173$$

$$\text{est } R^{*2} = 1 - \frac{(1-R^2)(N-1)}{(N-p-1)} = 1 - \frac{(1-.173)(14)}{(15-4-1)} = -.158$$

Since a squared value cannot be negative, we will declare it undefined. This is all the more reasonable in light of the fact that we cannot reject $H_0 : R^* = 0$.

15.15 Using the first three variables from Exercise 15.4:

a. Figure comparable to Figure 15.1:

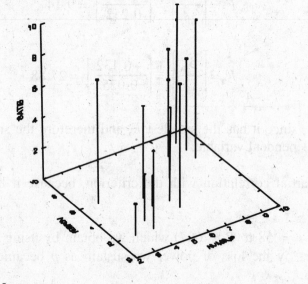

b.

$$\hat{Y} = 0.4067\text{Respon} + 0.1845\text{NumSup} + 2.3542$$

The slope of the plane with respect to the Respon axis $(X_1) = .4067$
The slope of the plane with respect to the NumSup axis $(X_2) = .1845$
The plane intersects the Y axis at 2.3542

15.17 It has no meaning in that we have the data for the population of interest (the 10 districts).

98

15.19 It plays a major role through its correlation with the residual components of the other variables.

15.21 Within the context of a multiple-regression equation, we cannot look at one variable alone. The slope for one variable is only the slope for that variable when all other variables are held constant. The percentage of mothers not seeking care until the third trimester is correlated with a number of other variables.

15.23 Create set of data examining residuals.

15.25 Rerun of Exercise 15.24 adding PVTotal.

b. The value of R^2 was virtually unaffected. However, the standard error of the regression coefficient for PVLoss increased from 0.105 to 0.178. Tolerance for PVLoss decreased from .981 to .345, whereas VIF increased from 1.019 to 2.900. **(c)** PVTotal should not be included in the model because it is redundant with the other variables.

15.27 Path diagram showing the relationships among the variables in the model.

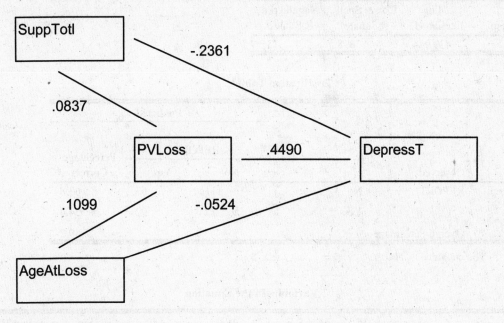

15.29 Regression diagnostics.

Case # 104 has the largest value of Cook's D (.137) but not a very large Studentized residual ($t = -1.88$). When we delete this case the squared multiple correlation is increased slightly. More importantly, the standard error of regression and the standard error of one of the predictors (PVLoss) also decrease slightly. This case is not sufficiently extreme to have a major impact on the data.

99

15.31 Logistic regression using Harass.dat:

The dependent variable (Reporting) is the last variable in the data set.

I cannot provide all possible models, so I am including just the most complete. This is a less than optimal model, but it provides a good starting point. This result was given by SPSS.

Block 1: Method = Enter

Omnibus Tests of Model Coefficients

		Chi-square	df	Sig.
Step 1	Step	35.442	5	.000
	Block	35.442	5	.000
	Model	35.442	5	.000

Model Summary

Step	-2 Log likelihood	Cox & Snell R Square	Nagelkerke R Square
1	439.984	.098	.131

Classification Table[a]

			Predicted		
			REPORT		Percentage
Observed			No	Yes	Correct
Step 1	REPORT	No	111	63	63.8
		Yes	77	92	54.4
	Overall Percentage				59.2

a. The cut value is .500

Variables in the Equation

		B	S.E.	Wald	df	Sig.	Exp(B)
Step 1[a]	AGE	-.014	.013	1.126	1	.289	.986
	MARSTAT	-.072	.234	.095	1	.757	.930
	FEMIDEOL	.007	.015	.228	1	.633	1.007
	FREQBEH	-.046	.153	.093	1	.761	.955
	OFFENSIV	.488	.095	26.431	1	.000	1.629
	Constant	-1.732	1.430	1.467	1	.226	.177

a. Variable(s) entered on step 1: AGE, MARSTAT, FEMIDEOL, FREQBEH, OFFENSIV.

From this set of predictors we see that overall $\chi^2_{LR} = 35.44$, which is significant on 5 df with a p value of .0000 (to 4 decimal places). The only predictor that contributes significantly is the Offensiveness of the behavior, which has a Wald χ^2 of 26.43. The exponentiation of the regression coefficient yields 0.9547. This would suggest that as the offensiveness of the behavior increases, the likelihood of reporting *decreases*. That's an odd result. But remember that we have all variables in the model. If we simply predicting reporting by using Offensiveness, $\exp(B) = 1.65$, which means that a 1 point increase in Offensiveness multiplies the odds of reporting by 1.65. Obviously we have some work to do to make sense of these data. I leave that to you.

15.33 It may well be that the frequency of the behavior is tied in with its offensiveness, which is related to the likelihood of reporting. In fact, the correlation between those two variables is .20, which is significant at $p < .000$. (I think my explanation would be more convincing if Frequency were a significant predictor when used on its own.)

15.35 BlamPer and BlamBeh are correlated at a moderate level ($r = .52$), and once we condition on BlamPer by including it in the equation, there is little left for BlamBeh to explain.

15.37 Make up an example.

15.39 This should cause them to pause. It is impossible to change one of the variables without changing the interaction in which that variable plays a role. In other words, I can't think of a sensible interpretation of "holding all other variables constant" in this situation.

15.41 Analysis of results from Feinberg and Willer (2011).

The following comes from using the program by Preacher and Leonardelli referred to in the chapter. I calculated the t values from the regression coefficients and their standard errors and then inserted those t values in the program. You can see that the mediated path is statistically significant regardless of which standard error you use for that path.

Input:	Test statistic:	p-value:
t_a 2.27	Sobel test: 2.0597124	0.03942604
t_b -4.90	Aroian test: 2.02528147	0.04283847
	Goodman test: 2.09596126	0.03608563
	Reset all	Calculate

Chapter 16 - Analyses of Variance and Covariance as General Linear Models

16.1 Eye fixations per line of text for poor, average, and good readers:

a. Design matrix, using only the first subject in each group:

$$X = \begin{bmatrix} 1 & 0 \\ 0 & 1 \\ -1 & -1 \end{bmatrix}$$

b. Computer exercise:

$$R^2 = .608 \quad SS_{reg} = 57.7333 \quad SS_{residual} = 37.2000$$

c. Analysis of variance:

$$\bar{X}_1 = 8.2000 \quad \bar{X}_2 = 5.6 \quad \bar{X}_3 = 3.4 \quad \bar{X}_. = 5.733$$

$$n_1 = 5 \quad n_2 = 5 \quad n_3 = 5 \quad N = 15 \quad \Sigma X = 86 \quad \Sigma X^2 = 588$$

$$SS_{total} = \Sigma X^2 - \frac{(\Sigma X)^2}{N} = 588 - \frac{86^2}{15} = 94.933$$

$$SS_{group} = n\Sigma(\bar{X}_j - \bar{X}_.)^2 = 5[(8.2000 - 5.733)^2 + (5.6 - 5.733)^2 + (3.4 - 5.733)^2]$$

$$= 57.733$$

$$SS_{error} = SS_{total} - SS_{group} = 94.933 - 57.733 = 37.200$$

Source	df	SS	MS	F
Group	2	57.733	28.867	9.312*
Error	12	37.200	3.100	
Total	14	94.933		

$*p < .05 \quad [F_{.05(2,12)} = 3.89]$

16.3 Data from Exercise 16.1, modified to make unequal ns:

$$R^2 = .624 \quad SS_{reg} = 79.0095 \quad SS_{residual} = 47.6571$$

Analysis of variance:

$$\bar{X}_1 = 8.2000 \quad \bar{X}_2 = 5.8571 \quad \bar{X}_3 = 3.3333 \quad \bar{X}_. = 5.7968$$

$$n_1 = 5 \quad n_2 = 7 \quad n_3 = 9 \quad N = 21 \quad \Sigma X = 112 \quad \Sigma X^2 = 724$$

$$SS_{total} = \sum X^2 - \frac{(\sum X)^2}{N} = 724 - \frac{112^2}{21} = 126.6666$$

$$SS_{group} = \sum n_j \left(\bar{X}_j - \bar{X}_. \right)^2 = 5[(8.2000 - 5.7968)^2 + 7(5.8571 - 5.7968)^2 + 9(3.3333 - 5.7968)^2]$$
$$= 79.0095$$

$$SS_{error} = SS_{total} - SS_{group} = 126.6666 - 79.0095 = 47.6571$$

Source	df	SS	MS	F
Group	2	79.0095	39.5048	14.92*
Error	18	47.6571	2.6476	
Total	20	126.6666		

$*p < .05 \quad [F_{.05(2,18)} = 3.55]$

16.5 Relationship between Gender, SES, and Locus of Control:

a. Analysis of Variance:

		SES			
		Low	Average	High	Mean
Gender	Male	12.25	14.25	17.25	14.583
	Female	8.25	12.25	16.25	12.250
	Mean	10.25	13.25	16.75	13.417

$\Sigma X = 644 \quad \Sigma X^2 = 9418 \quad n = 8 \quad N = 48$

103

$$SS_{total} = \Sigma X^2 - \frac{(\Sigma X)^2}{N} = 9418 - \frac{644^2}{48} = 777.6667$$

$$SS_{gender} = sn\Sigma\left(\bar{X}_{i.} - \bar{X}_{..}\right)^2 = 3(8)[(14.583-13.417)^2 + (12.250-13.417)^2]$$
$$= 65.333$$

$$SS_{SES} = gn\Sigma\left(\bar{X}_{.j} - \bar{X}_{..}\right)^2 = 2(8)[(10.25-13.417)^2 + (13.25-13.417)^2 + (16.75-13.417)^2]$$
$$= 338.6667$$

$$SS_{cells} = n\Sigma\left(\bar{X}_{ij} - \bar{X}_{..}\right)^2 = 8[(12.25-13.417)^2 + ... + (16.25-13.417)^2] = 422.6667$$

$$SS_{GS} = SS_{cells} - SS_{gender} - SS_{SES} = 422.6667 - 65.3333 - 338.6667 = 18.6667$$

$$SS_{error} = SS_{total} - SS_{cells} = 777.6667 - 422.6667 = 355.0000$$

Source	df	SS	MS	F
Gender	1	65.333	65.333	7.730*
SES	2	338.667	169.333	20.034*
G x S	2	18.667	9.333	1.104
Error	42	355.000	8.452	
Total	47	777.667		

$*p < .05$ $[F_{.05(1,42)} = 4.08; F_{.05(2,42)} = 3.23]$

b. ANOVA summary table constructed from sums of squares calculated from design matrix:

$$SS_G = SS_{reg(\alpha,\beta,\alpha\beta)} - SS_{reg(\beta,\alpha\beta)} = 422.6667 - 357.3333 = 65.333$$

$$SS_S = SS_{reg(\alpha,\beta,\alpha\beta)} - SS_{reg(\alpha,\alpha\beta)} = 422.6667 - 84.0000 = 338.667$$

$$SS_{GS} = SS_{reg(\alpha,\beta,\alpha\beta)} - SS_{reg(\alpha,\beta)} = 422.6667 - 404.000 = 18.667$$

$$SS_{total} = SS_Y = 777.667$$

The summary table is exactly the same as in part a (above).

104

16.7 The data from Exercise 16.5 modified to make unequal ns:

$$SS_{error} = SS_Y - SS_{reg(\alpha,\beta,\alpha\beta)} = 750.1951 - 458.7285 = 291.467$$

$$SS_G = SS_{reg(\alpha,\beta,\alpha\beta)} - SS_{reg(\beta,\alpha\beta))} = 458.7285 - 398.7135 = 60.015$$

$$SS = SS_{reg(\alpha,\beta,\alpha\beta)} - SS_{reg(\alpha,\alpha\beta)} = 458.7285 - 112.3392 = 346.389$$

$$SS = SS_{reg(\alpha,\beta,\alpha\beta)} - SS_{reg(\alpha,\beta)} = 458.7285 - 437.6338 = 21.095$$

Source	df	SS	MS	F
Gender	1	60.015	60.015	7.21*
SES	2	346.389	173.195	20.80*
G x S	2	21.095	10.547	1.27
Error	35	291.467	8.328	
Total	40			

$*p < .05 \quad [F_{.05(1,35)} = 4.12; F_{.05(2,35)} = 3.27]$

16.9 Model from data in Exercise 16.5:

$$1.1667A_1 - 3.1667B_1 - 0.1667B_2 + 0.8333AB_{11} - 0.1667AB_{12} + 13.4167$$

Means:

		Low	Avg	High	
Gender (A)	Male	12.25	14.25	17.25	14.583
	Female	8.25	12.25	16.25	12.250

SES (B)

$\hat{\mu} = \overline{X}.. = 13.4167 = b_0 = $ intercept

$\hat{\alpha}_1 = \overline{A}_1 - \overline{X}.. = 14.583 - 13.4167 = 1.1667 = b_1$

$\hat{\beta}_1 = \overline{B}_1 - \overline{X}.. = 10.25 - 13.4167 = -3.1667 = b_2$

$\hat{\beta}_2 = \overline{B}_2 - \overline{X}.. = 13.25 - 13.4167 = -0.1667 = b_3$

$\widehat{\alpha\beta}_{11} = \overline{AB}_{11} - \overline{A}_1 - \overline{B}_1 + \overline{X}.. = 12.25 - 14.583 - 10.25 + 13.1467 = 0.8337 = b_4$

$\widehat{\alpha\beta}_{12} = \overline{AB}_{12} - \overline{A}_1 - \overline{B}_2 + \overline{X}.. = 14.25 - 14.583 - 13.25 + 13.1467 = -0.1667 = b_5$

16.11 Does Method III really deal with unweighted means?

Means:

	B_1	B_2	weighted	unweighted
A_1	4	10	8.5	7.0
A_2	10	4	8.0	7.0
weighted	8.0	8.5	8.29	
unweighted	7.0	7.0		7.0

The full model produced by Method 1: $\hat{Y} = 0.0A_1 + 0.0B_1 - 3.0AB_{11} + 7.0$

Effects calculated on weighted means:

$$\hat{\mu} = \overline{X}.. = 8.29 = b_0 \neq \text{intercept}$$

$$\hat{\alpha}_1 = \overline{A}_1 - \overline{X}.. = 8.50 - 8.29 = 0.21 \neq b_1$$

$$\hat{\beta}_1 = \overline{B}_1 - \overline{X}.. = 8.00 - 8.29 = 0.29 \neq b_2$$

$$\widehat{\alpha\beta}_{11} = \overline{AB}_{11} - \overline{A}_1 - \overline{B}_1 + \overline{X}.. = 4.00 - 8.50 - 8.00 + 8.29 = -4.21 \neq b_3$$

Effects calculated on unweighted means:

$$\hat{\mu} = \overline{X}.. = 7.00 = b_0 = \text{intercept}$$

$$\hat{\alpha}_1 = \overline{A}_1 - \overline{X}.. = 7.00 - 7.00 = 0.00 = b_1$$

$$\hat{\beta}_1 = \overline{B}_1 - \overline{X}.. = 7.00 - 7.00 = 0.00 = b_2$$

$$\widehat{\alpha\beta}_{11} = \overline{AB}_{11} - \overline{A}_1 - \overline{B}_1 + \overline{X}.. = 4.00 - 7.00 - 7.00 + 7.00 = -3.00 = b_3$$

These coefficients found by the model clearly reflect the effects computed on unweighted means. Alternately, carrying out the complete analysis leads to $SS_A = SS_B = 0.00$, again reflecting equality of unweighted means.

16.13 Venn diagram representing the sums of squares in Exercise 16.7:

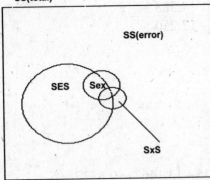

16.15 Energy consumption of families:

a. Design matrix, using only the first entry in each group for illustration purposes:

$$X = \begin{bmatrix} 1 & 0 & 58 & 75 \\ \cdots & \cdots & \cdots & \cdots \\ 0 & 1 & 60 & 70 \\ \cdots & \cdots & \cdots & \cdots \\ -1 & -1 & 75 & 80 \end{bmatrix}$$

b. Analysis of covariance:

$$SS_{reg(\alpha,cov,\alpha c)} = 2424.6202$$

$$SS_{reg(\alpha,cov)} = 2369.2112$$

$$SS_{residual} = 246.5221 = SS_{error}$$

There is not a significant decrement in SS_{reg} and thus we can continue to assume homogeneity of regression.

$$SS_{reg(\alpha)} = 1118.5333$$

$$SS_{cov} = SS_{reg(\alpha,cov)} - SS_{reg(\alpha)} = 2369.2112 - 1118.5333 = 1250.6779$$

$$SS_{reg(cov)} = 1716.2884$$

$$SS_A = SS_{reg(\alpha,cov)} - SS_{reg(cov)} = 2369.2112 - 1716.2884 = 652.9228$$

Source	df	SS	MS	F
Covariate	1	1250.6779	1250.6779	55.81*
A (Group)	2	652.9228	326.4614	14.57*
Error	11	246.5221	22.4111	
Total	14	2615.7333		

$*p < .05$ $[F_{.05(1,11)} = 4.84; F_{.05(2,11)} = 3.98]$

16.17 Adjusted means for the data in Exercise 16.16:

(The order of the means may differ depending on how you code the group membership and how the software sets up its design matrix. But the numerical values should agree.)

$$\hat{Y} = -7.9099 A_1 + 0.8786 A_2 - 2.4022 B_1 + 0.5667 AB_{11} + 0.1311 AB_{21} + 0.7260 C + 6.3740$$

$$\hat{Y}_{11} = -7.9099(1) + 0.8786(0) - 2.4022(1) + 0.5667(1) + 0.1311(0)$$
$$+ 0.7260(61.3333) + 6.3740 = 41.1566$$

$$\hat{Y}_{12} = -7.9099(1) + 0.8786(0) - 2.4022(-1) + 0.5667(-1) + 0.1311(0)$$
$$+ 0.7260(61.3333) + 6.3740 = 44.8276$$

$$\hat{Y}_{21} = -7.9099(0) + 0.8786(1) - 2.4022(1) + 0.5667(0) + 0.1311(1)$$
$$+ 0.7260(61.3333) + 6.3740 = 49.5095$$

$$\hat{Y}_{22} = -7.9099(0) + 0.8786(1) - 2.4022(-1) + 0.5667(0) + 0.1311(-1)$$
$$+ 0.7260(61.3333) + 6.3740 = 54.0517$$

$$\hat{Y}_{31} = -7.9099(-1) + 0.8786(-1) - 2.4022(1) + 0.5667(-1) + 0.1311(-1)$$
$$+ 0.7260(61.3333) + 6.3740 = 54.8333$$

$$\hat{Y}_{32} = -7.9099(-1) + 0.8786(-1) - 2.4022(-1) + 0.5667(1) + 0.1311(1)$$
$$+ 0.7260(61.3333) + 6.3740 = 61.0333$$

(We enter 61.3333 for the covariate in each case, because we want to estimate what the cell means would be if the observations in those cells were always at the mean of the covariate.)

16.19 Klemchuk, Bond, & Howell (1990)

Tests of Between-Subjects Effects

Dependent Variable:DV

Source	Type III Sum of Squares	df	Mean Square	F	Sig.
Corrected Model	15.728[a]	3	5.243	8.966	.000
Intercept	2.456	1	2.456	4.201	.048
Daycare	2.640	1	2.640	4.515	.041
Age	11.703	1	11.703	20.016	.000
Daycare * Age	.037	1	.037	.064	.802
Error	21.050	36	.585		
Total	46.111	40			
Corrected Total	36.778	39			

a. R Squared = .428 (Adjusted R Squared = .380)

16.21 Analysis of GSIT in Mireault.dat:

Tests of Between-Subjects Effects

Dependent Variable: GSIT

Source	Type III Sum of Squares	df	Mean Square	F	Sig.
Corrected Model	1216.924[a]	5	243.385	2.923	.013
Intercept	1094707.516	1	1094707.516	13146.193	.000
GENDER	652.727	1	652.727	7.839	.005
GROUP	98.343	2	49.172	.590	.555
GENDER * GROUP	419.722	2	209.861	2.520	.082
Error	30727.305	369	83.272		
Total	1475553.000	375			
Corrected Total	31944.229	374			

a. R Squared = .038 (Adjusted R Squared = .025)

Estimated Marginal Means

GENDER * GROUP

Dependent Variable: GSIT

GENDER	GROUP	Mean	Std. Error	95% Confidence Interval Lower Bound	Upper Bound
Male	1	62.367	1.304	59.804	64.931
	2	64.676	1.107	62.500	66.853
	3	63.826	1.903	60.084	67.568
Female	1	62.535	.984	60.600	64.470
	2	60.708	.858	59.020	62.396
	3	58.528	1.521	55.537	61.518

16.23 Analysis of variance on the covariate from Exercise 16.22.

The following is abbreviated SAS output.

```
                    General Linear Models Procedure


Dependent Variable: YEARCOLL

                                    Sum of          Mean
Source                  DF          Squares         Square      F Value     Pr > F
Model                   5           13.3477645      2.6695529   2.15        0.0600
Error                   292         363.0012288     1.2431549
Corrected Total         297         376.3489933


                    R-Square            C.V.            Root MSE        YEARCOLL Mean
                    0.035466            41.53258        1.11497         2.6845638


Source                  DF          Type III SS     Mean Square     F Value   Pr > F
```

109

GENDER	1	5.95006299	5.95006299	4.79	0.0295
GROUP	2	0.78070431	0.39035216	0.31	0.7308
GENDER*GROUP	2	2.96272310	1.48136155	1.19	0.3052

GENDER	GROUP	YEARCOLL LSMEAN
1	1	2.27906977
1	2	2.53225806
1	3	2.68421053
2	1	2.88888889
2	2	2.85000000
2	3	2.70967742

These data reveal a significant difference between males and females in terms of YearColl. Females are slightly ahead of males. If the first year of college is in fact more stressful than later years, this could account for some of the difference we found in Exercise 16.21.

16.25 Everitt compared two therapy groups and a control group treatment for anorexia. The groups differed significantly in posttest weight when controlling for pretest weight ($F = 8.71, p < .0001$, with the Control group weighing the least at posttest. When we examine the difference between just the two treatment groups at posttest, the F does not reach significant, $F = 3.745, p = .060$, though the effect size for the difference between means (again controlling for pretest weights) is 0.62 with the Family Therapy group weighing about six pounds more than the Cognitive/Behavior Therapy group. It is difficult to know just how to interpret that result given the nonsignificant F.

16.27 A slope of 1.0 would mean that the treatment added a constant to people's pretest scores, which seems somewhat unlikely. Students might try taking any of the data in the book with a pretest and posttest score and plotting the relationship.

This relationship between difference scores and the analysis of covariance would suggest that in general an analysis of covariance might be the preferred approach. The only time I might think otherwise is when the difference score is really the measure of interest.

Chapter 17 – Meta-Analysis and Single-Case Designs

[Note: The exercises in this chapter come as groups of exercises on a common research study. It is sometimes difficult to separate the answers neatly by individual question. For that reason I will make an exception in this chapter and provide general answers without trying to restrict them to the odd-numbered items.]

17.1 Mazzucchelli et al. (2010) study

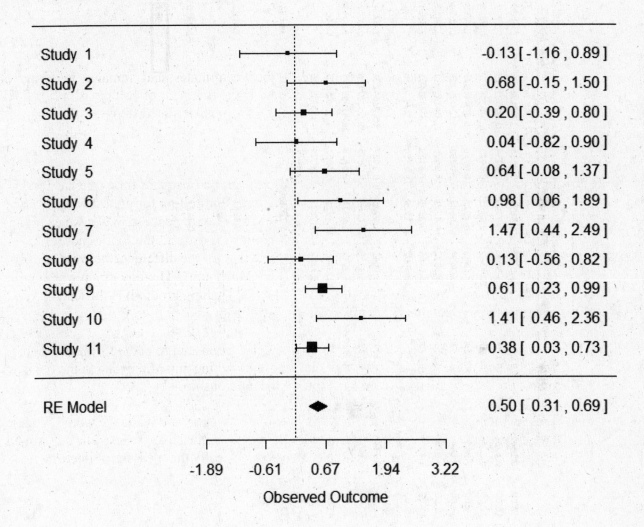

Author	SubGrp	n1	n2	g	sg^2	weight	Wg	W*g^2	W^2	W(gi-gbar)^2
Barlow86a	E	12.00	12.00	-0.134	0.2740	3.6496	-0.4891	0.0655	13.3198359	1.4609
Besyner79	E	14.00	16.00	0.675	0.1790	5.5866	3.7709	2.5454	31.21001217	0.1737
Lovett88	E	33.00	27.00	0.204	0.0930	10.7527	2.1935	0.4475	115.6203029	0.9338
Stark	E	10.00	9.00	0.043	0.1930	5.1813	0.2228	0.0096	26.84635829	1.0759
VanDenHaut	E	15.00	14.00	0.644	0.1380	7.2464	4.6667	3.0053	52.5099769	0.1530
Weinberg	E	10.00	9.00	0.976	0.2180	4.5872	4.4771	4.3696	21.04199983	1.0451
Wilson	E	9.00	11.00	1.456	0.2750	3.6364	5.3309	7.8151	13.2231405	3.4025
SUM		103.00	98.00			40.6402	20.1729	18.2580	273.7716	
Barlow86a	M	12.00	13.00	0.133	0.1240	8.0645	1.0726	0.1427	65.0364204	1.0784
Fordyce77	M	50.00	60.00	0.609	0.0380	26.3158	16.0263	9.7600	692.5207756	0.3202
Fordyce83	M	40.00	13.00	1.41	0.2330	4.2918	6.0515	8.5326	18.41993774	3.5644
Reich81	M	49.00	49.00	0.378	0.0320	31.2500	11.8125	4.4651	976.5625	0.4552
SUM		151.00	135.00			69.9222	34.9629	22.9004	1752.5396	
GrandSum		254.00	233.00			110.5623	55.1358		2026.3113	13.6631

Mean g = 0.4987
se(Mean g) = 0.0951

Q = 13.6631 which is chi.sq on 10 df
p = .189

CI-lower = 0.3123
CI-upper = 0.6851

C = 92.2350

Tau = 0.1993

17.5 Fixed model

Fixed-Effects Model (k = 11)

Test for Heterogeneity:
Q(df = 10) = 13.6678, p-val = 0.1887

Model Results:

estimate	se	zval	pval	ci.lb	ci.ub	
0.4987	0.0951	5.2428	<.0001	0.3122	0.6851	***

Signif. codes: 0 '***' 0.001 '**' 0.01 '*' 0.05 '.' 0.1 ' ' 1

17.6 - 17.8 The following results are from R using library(metaphor)

Fixed-Effects Model (k = 4)

Test for Heterogeneity:
Q(df = 3) = 7.2655, p-val = 0.0639

Model Results:

estimate	se	zval	pval	ci.lb	ci.ub	
0.2274	0.0881	2.5813	0.0098	0.0547	0.4001	**

Signif. codes: 0 '***' 0.001 '**' 0.01 '*' 0.05 '.' 0.1 ' ' 1

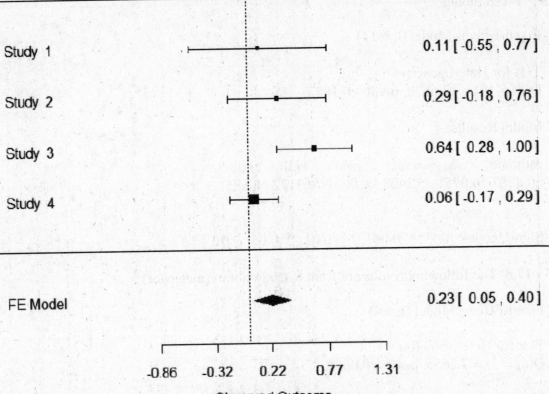

It doesn't make sense to try to fit a random model because we have so few studies that we could not reasonably test for randomness.

17.9 The confidence interval does not include 0, and we can safely reject the null hypothesis and conclude that methylphenidate does increase the severity of tics in these children.

17.10 - 17.12

Fixed-Effects Model (k = 3)

Test for Heterogeneity:
Q(df = 2) = 2.1121, p-val = 0.3478

Model Results:

estimate	se	zval	pval	ci.lb	ci.ub	
0.7364	0.0955	7.7109	<.0001	0.5492	0.9236	***

Signif. codes: 0 '***' 0.001 '**' 0.01 '*' 0.05 '.' 0.1 ' ' 1

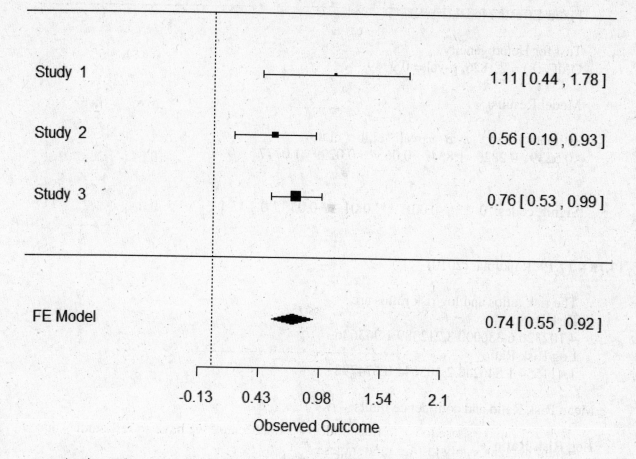

Again we have too few studies to seriously look at heterogeneity.

17.13 – 17.14

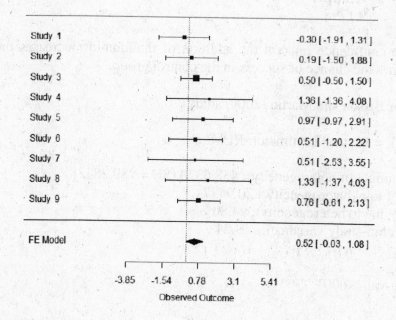

Fixed-Effects Model (k = 9)

Test for Heterogeneity:
$Q(df = 8) = 2.1826$, p-val = 0.9749

Model Results:

estimate	se	zval	pval	ci.lb	ci.ub
0.5239	0.2826	1.8542	0.0637	-0.0299	1.0777

Signif. codes: 0 '***' 0.001 '**' 0.01 '*' 0.05 '.' 0.1 ' ' 1

17.15 – 17.19 Rajkumar (2010)

The risk ratios and log risk ratios are
Risk Ratio
4.102326 6.336000 8.212389 1.963636
Log Risk Ratio
1.411554 1.846248 2.105644 0.674798

Mean Risk Ratio and confidence limits

Log Risk Ratio

Estimate	se	zval	pval	ci.lb	ci.ub
1.5747	0.3277	4.8055	<.0001	0.9324	2.2170

Risk Ratio	**CIlower**	**CIupper**
4.8293	2.5406	9.1798

Even at the low end of the confidence interval the addition of thalidomide increases the chances of success to 2.5 times the chance of success in the control group.

17.20 Random effects model for Bisson and Martin (2009) study

Random-Effects Model (k = 14; tau^2 estimator: REML)

tau^2 (estimate of total amount of heterogeneity): 438.6370 (SE = 189.2833)
tau (sqrt of the estimate of total heterogeneity): 20.9437
I^2 (% of total variability due to heterogeneity): 94.80%
H^2 (total variability / within-study variance): 19.24

Test for Heterogeneity:
$Q(df = 13) = 236.1772$, p-val < .0001

116

Model Results:

estimate	se	zval	pval	ci.lb	ci.ub	
-28.6212	5.8774	-4.8697	<.0001	-40.1407	-17.1017	***

Study 1	-56.10 [-64.59 , -47.61]
Study 2	-14.33 [-19.26 , -9.40]
Study 3	-66.00 [-81.93 , -50.07]
Study 4	-46.73 [-54.09 , -39.37]
Study 5	-31.00 [-45.00 , -17.00]
Study 6	-4.10 [-12.29 , 4.09]
Study 7	-3.10 [-21.43 , 15.23]
Study 8	-52.97 [-70.97 , -34.97]
Study 9	-5.50 [-12.47 , 1.47]
Study 10	-10.20 [-23.66 , 3.26]
Study 11	-30.30 [-44.62 , -15.98]
Study 12	-37.10 [-61.38 , -12.82]
Study 13	-6.00 [-13.07 , 1.07]
Study 14	-43.30 [-56.46 , -30.14]
RE Model	-28.62 [-40.14 , -17.10]

-101.36   -67.36   -33.35   0.65   34.66

Mean Difference

Note that we can reject the null hypothesis in our test for heterogeneity, though we have no specific variable that might explain that variability. We can also conclude that VBT is a more effective treatment than the Control treatment.

117

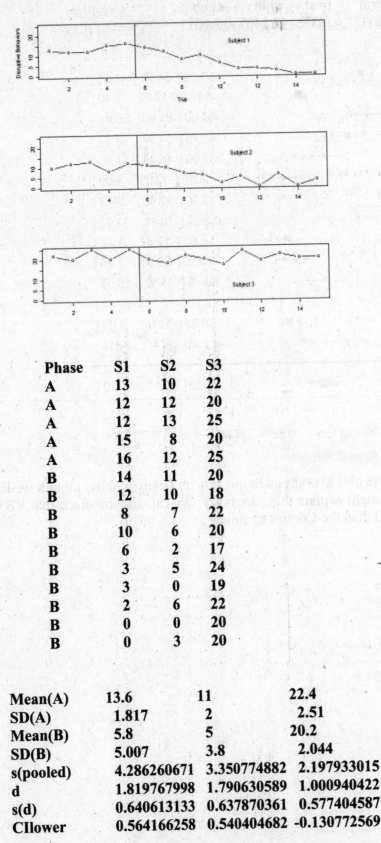

Phase	S1	S2	S3
A	13	10	22
A	12	12	20
A	12	13	25
A	15	8	20
A	16	12	25
B	14	11	20
B	12	10	18
B	8	7	22
B	10	6	20
B	6	2	17
B	3	5	24
B	3	0	19
B	2	6	22
B	0	0	20
B	0	3	20

Mean(A)	13.6	11	22.4
SD(A)	1.817	2	2.51
Mean(B)	5.8	5	20.2
SD(B)	5.007	3.8	2.044
s(pooled)	4.286260671	3.350774882	2.197933015
d	1.819767998	1.790630589	1.000940422
s(d)	0.640613133	0.637870361	0.577404587
CIlower	0.564166258	0.540404682	-0.130772569

118

CIupper	3.075369738	3.040856496	2.132653414	
Weight	2.436735134	2.457735569	2.999435588	7.893906291
Widi	4.434292616	4.40089649	3.002256323	11.83744543

dbar	1.499567514
s(dbar)	0.355921331
CIlow(dbar)	0.801961705
CIup(dbar)	2.197173322

Two of the three subjects showed significant improvement (their confidence intervals did not include 0, and the overall confidence interval also did not include 0, indicating significant overall improvement.

17.25 – 17.28

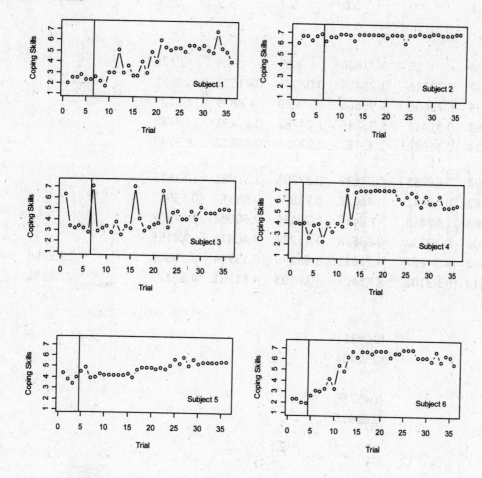

	Subj1	Subj2	Subj3	Subj4	Subj5	Subj6
	2.0	6	6.3	4.0	4.4	2.3
	2.5	6.7	3.4	3.9	3.8	2.3
	2.5	6.7	3.2	4.0	3.4	2.0
	2.8	6.3	3.4	2.6	4.0	1.9
	2.3	6.7	3.2	3.8	4.5	2.6
	2.3	6.9	2.8	3.9	4.9	3.1
	2.6	6.2	7.1	2.3	3.9	3.0
	2.2	6.6	2.9	4.0	4.0	3.3

The Rest Of The Data Go Here

	Subj1	Subj2	Subj3	Subj4	Subj5	Subj6
	6.9	6.9	4.7	5.5	5.4	5.8
	5.3	6.9	5.0	5.5	5.4	6.4
	5.0	7.0	5.1	5.6	5.5	6.3
	4.1	7.0	5.0	5.7	5.5	5.6

	Subj1	Subj2	Subj3	Subj4	Subj5	Subj6	
Mean(A)	2.4	6.55	3.71666	3.95	3.9	2.125	
SD(A)	0.26832	0.33316	1.28439	0.07071	0.41633	0.20615	
Mean(B)	4.35	6.76666	4.96666	4.29	4.8875	4.5125	
SD(B)	1.76493	0.31411	1.33516	1.24762	0.67493	1.64788	
s(pooled)	1.63324	0.31698	1.32782	1.23218	0.65622	1.5747	
d	-1.19394	-0.68352	-0.94139	-0.27593	-1.50481	-1.51616	
s(d)	0.46882	0.45441	0.46077	0.72894	0.55919	0.55962	
CIlower	2.11284	1.57416	-1.8445	1.70466	2.60084	2.61302	
CIupper	0.27504	0.20712	-0.03828	1.15279	0.40879	-0.4193	
Weight	4.54962	4.84287	4.71012	1.88196	3.19794	3.19308	22.3756
Widi	-5.4319	-3.3102	-4.43407	-0.5193	4.81231	4.84123	23.3491

dbar	-1.04351
s(dbar)	0.211404
CIlow(dbar)	-1.45786
CIup(dbar)	-0.62915

17.29 – 17.31

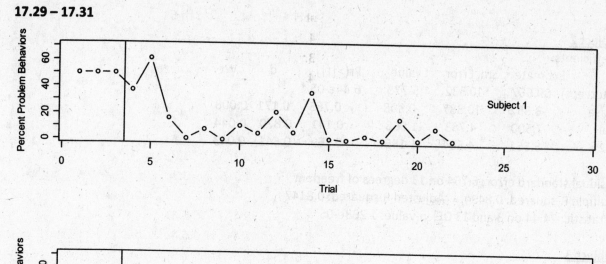

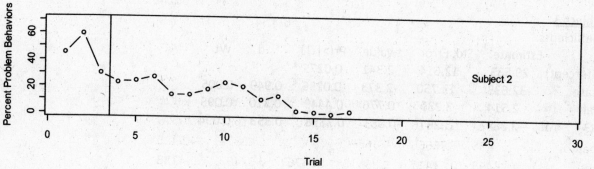

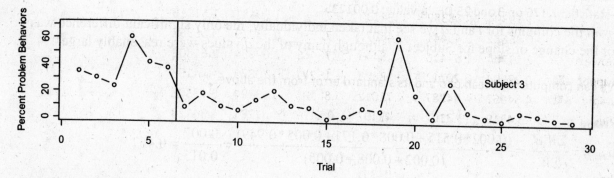

Individual Regressions

Subject 1
Coefficients:

	Estimate	Std. Error	t value	Pr(>|t|)	d	Wt
(Intercept)	5.000e+01	2.182e+01	2.291	0.0342 *		
Phase	-2.482e+01	2.272e+01	-1.092	0.2891	0.515	0.002
trial	-7.106e-15	1.010e+01	0.000	1.0000	0.000	0.010
int1	-1.447e+00	1.012e+01	-0.143	0.8879	0.943	0.010

Residual standard error: 14.29 on 18 degrees of freedom
Multiple R-squared: 0.5717,   Adjusted R-squared: 0.5003
F-statistic: 8.008 on 3 and 18 DF, p-value: 0.000

Subject 2
Coefficients:

	Estimate	Std. Error	t value	Pr(>|t|)	d	Wt
(Intercept)	59.667	10.332	5.775	6.44e-05 *		
Phase	-3.352	10.887	-0.308	0.763	0.171	0.008
trial	-7.500	4.783	-1.568	0.141	0.870	0.044
int2	5.551	4.804	1.155	0.269	0.641	0.043

Residual standard error: 6.764 on 13 degrees of freedom
Multiple R-squared: 0.8494,   Adjusted R-squared: 0.8147
F-statistic: 24.44 on 3 and 13 DF,   p-value: 1.283e-05

Subject 3
Coefficients:

	Estimate	Std. Error	t value	Pr(>|t|)	d	Wt
(Intercept)	29.533	12.614	2.341	0.0275 *		
Phase	-32.633	13.750	-2.373	0.0256 *	0.949	0.005
trial	2.514	3.239	0.776	0.4449	0.310	0.095
int3	-2.884	3.267	-0.883	0.3858	0.353	0.094

Residual standard error: 13.55 on 25 degrees of freedom
Multiple R-squared: 0.4627,   Adjusted R-squared: 0.3982
F-statistic: 7.176 on 3 and 25 DF,   p-value: 0.001235

From the columns for t and d we see that taken individually, the only significant difference was for the change of slope for Subject 3, although many of the d values were reasonably large.

We can compute the mean of d and its standard error from the above.

Phase

$$\bar{d}_{Phase} = \frac{\Sigma W_i d_1}{\Sigma W_i} = \frac{(0.002 * 0.515 + 0.008 * 0.171 + 0.005 * 0.949)}{(0.002 + 0.008 + 0.005)} = \frac{0.007}{0.015} = 0.467$$

$$s_{\bar{d}} = \sqrt{\frac{1}{\Sigma W_i}} = \sqrt{\frac{1}{0.015}} = 8.165$$

Trial

$$\bar{d}_{Trial} = \frac{0.068}{.149} = 0.046$$

$$s_{\bar{d}} = \sqrt{\frac{1}{0.149}} = 2.59$$

Interaction

$$\bar{d}_{int} = \frac{0.070}{0.147} = 0.476$$

$$s_{\bar{d}} = \sqrt{\frac{1}{0.147}} = 2.608$$

It is apparent from the above results that the mean of d is not significant for any effect. Contrary to the example in the text, the standard errors were very large.

Chapter 18 – Resampling and Nonparametric Approaches To Data

18.1 Inferences in children's story summaries (McConaughy, 1980):

a. Analysis using Wilcoxon's rank-sum test:

	Younger Children							Older Children					
Raw Data:	0	1	0	3	2	5	2	4	7	6	4	8	7
Ranks:	1.5	3	1.5	6	4.5	9	4.5	7.5	11.5	10	7.5	13	11.5

$\bullet R = 30$ $N = 7$ $\bullet R = 61$ $N = 6$

$$W_S = \Sigma R \text{ for group with smaller } N = 61$$
$$W_S' = 2\,\overline{W} - W_S = 84 - 61 = 23$$

$W'_S < W_S$, therefore use W'_S in Appendix W_S. Double the probability level for a 2-tailed test.

$$W_{.025\,(6,7)} = 27 > 23$$

b. Reject H_0 and conclude that older children include more inferences in their summaries.

18.3 The analysis in Exercise 18.2 using the normal approximation:

$$z = \frac{W_S - \dfrac{n_1(n_1+n_2+1)}{2}}{\sqrt{\dfrac{n_1 n_2(n_1+n_2+1)}{12}}} = \frac{53 - \dfrac{9(9+11+1)}{2}}{\sqrt{\dfrac{9(11)(9+11+1)}{12}}} = -3.15$$

z	p
3.00	.0013
3.15	.0009
3.25	.0006

$$p(z \geq \pm 3.15) = 2(.0009) = .0018 < .05$$

Reject H_0, which was the same conclusion as we came to in Exercise 18.2.

18.5 Hypothesis formation in psychiatric residents (Nurcombe & Fitzhenry-Coor, 1979):
a. Analysis using Wilcoxon's matched-pairs signed-ranks test:

Before:	8	4	2	2	4	8	3	1	3	9
After:	7	9	3	6	3	10	6	7	8	7
Difference:	-1	+5	+1	+4	-1	+2	+3	+6	+5	-2
Rank:	2	8.5	2	7	2	4.5	6	10	8.5	4.5
Signed Rank:	-2	8.5	2	7	-2	4.5	6	10	8.5	-4.5

$$T_+ = \Sigma(\text{positive ranks}) = 46.5$$

124

$$T_- = \Sigma(\text{negative ranks}) = 8.5$$
$$T = \text{smaller of } |T_+| \text{ or } |T-| = 8.5$$
$$T_{.025\,(10)} = 8 < 8.5 \quad \text{Do not reject } H_0.$$

b. We cannot conclude that we have evidence supporting the hypothesis that there is a reliable increase in hypothesis generation and testing over time. (Here is a case in which alternative methods of breaking ties could lead to different conclusions.)

18.7 I would randomly assign the two scores for each subject to the Before and After location, and calculate my test statistic (the sum of the negative differences) for each randomization. Having done that a large number of times, the distribution of the sum of negative differences would be the sampling distribution against which to compare my obtained result.

18.9 The analysis in Exercise 18.8 using the normal approximation:

$$z = \frac{T - \dfrac{n(n=1)}{4}}{\sqrt{\dfrac{n(n+1)(2n+1)}{24}}} = \frac{46 - \dfrac{20(20+1)}{4}}{\sqrt{\dfrac{20(20+1)(40+1)}{24}}} = -2.20$$

$$p(z \geq \pm 2.20) = 2(.0139) = .0278 < .05$$

Again reject H_0, which agrees with our earlier conclusion.

18.11 Data in Exercise 18.8 plotted as a function of first-born's score:

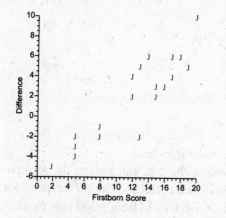

The scatter plot shows that the difference between the pairs is heavily dependent upon the score for the first born.

18.13 The Wilcoxon Matched-pairs signed-ranks test tests the null hypothesis that paired scores were drawn from identical populations or from symmetric populations with the same mean (and median). The corresponding t test tests the null hypothesis that the paired scores were drawn from populations with the same mean and assumes normality.

18.15 Rejection of H_0 by a t test is a more specific statement than rejection using the appropriate distribution-free test because, by making assumptions about normality and homogeneity of variance, the t test refers specifically to population means.

18.17 Truancy and home situation of delinquent adolescents:

Analysis using Kruskal-Wallis one-way analysis of variance:

Natural Home		Foster Home		Group Home	
Score	Rank	Score	Rank	Score	Rank
15	18	16	19	10	9
18	22	14	16	13	13.5
19	24.5	20	26	14	16
14	16	22	27	11	10
5	4.5	19	24.5	7	6.5
8	8	5	4.5	3	2
12	11.5	17	20	4	3
13	13.5	18	22	18	22
7	6.5	12	11.5	2	1

$R_i = 124.5 \quad 170.5 \quad 83 \qquad N = 27 \, n = 9$

$$H = \frac{12}{N(N+1)} \Sigma \frac{R_i^2}{n_i} - 3(N+1)$$

$$= \frac{12}{27(27+1)} \left[\frac{124.5^2}{9} + \frac{170.5^2}{9} + \frac{83^2}{9} \right] - 3(27+1)$$

$$= 6.757$$

$$\chi_{.05}^2(2) = 5.99 \quad Reject \, H_0$$

18.19 I would take the data from all of the groups and assign them at random to the groups. For each random assignment I would calculate a statistic that reflected the differences (or lack thereof) among the groups. The standard F statistic would be a good one to use. This randomization, repeated many times, will give me the sampling distribution of F, and that distribution does not depend on an assumption of normality. I could then compare the F that I obtained for my data against that sampling distribution. The result follows.

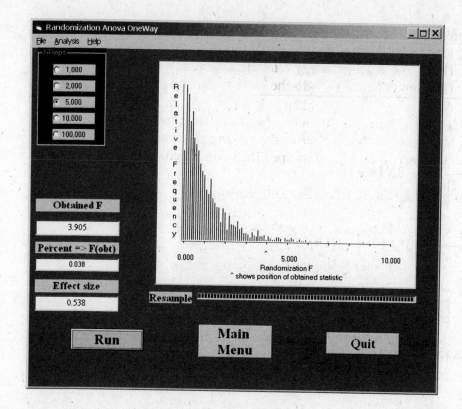

18.21 The study in Exercise 18.18 has the advantage over the one in Exercise 18.17 in that it eliminates the influence of individual differences (differences in overall level of truancy from one person to another).

18.23 For the data in Exercise 18.5:

a. Analyzed by chi-square:

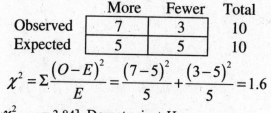

	More	Fewer	Total
Observed	7	3	10
Expected	5	5	10

$$\chi^2 = \Sigma \frac{(O-E)^2}{E} = \frac{(7-5)^2}{5} + \frac{(3-5)^2}{5} = 1.6$$

$[\chi^2_{.05(1)} = 3.84]$ Do not reject H_0

b. Analyzed by Friedman's test:

Before		After	
8	(2)	7	(1)
4	(1)	9	(2)
2	(1)	3	(2)
2	(1)	6	(2)
4	(2)	3	(1)
8	(1)	10	(2)
3	(1)	6	(2)

	Before		After	
1	(1)	7	(2)
3	(1)	8	(2)
9	(2)	7	(1)
	(13)		(17)

$N = 10 \qquad k = 2$

$$\chi_F^2 = \frac{12}{Nk(k+1)}\Sigma R_i^2 - 3N(k+1)$$

$$= \frac{12}{12(2)(2+1)}\left[13^2 + 17^2\right] - 3(10)(2+1)$$

$$= 1.6 \qquad \left[\chi_{.05}^2(2) = 5.99\right] \quad \text{Do not reject } H_0$$

These are exactly equivalent tests in this case.